THE
NATURE OF GOLF

EXPLORING THE BEAUTY OF THE GAME

THE
NATURE OF GOLF

EXPLORING THE BEAUTY OF THE GAME

THOMAS P. STEWART AND RUSSELL SHOEMAN
INTRODUCTION BY DOUG SANDERS

Thomas P. Stewart

Design: Natalie Pere, Derek Barnes

Research: Chriss Szabo

Principal Photography: Karen Louis, Russell Shoeman, Patricia Holdsworth

Other Photographic Contributors: Wintergreen Resort, 3, 14, 23, 32; Betty Anne Hopke, 5, 17; Ken Lawless, 7; Janice Hopkins-Snably, 20, 26, 31, 32, 65, 280; Amelia Island Plantation, 39, 41, 47; William Raser, 54, 55; The BALSAMS, 59, 62; Lois Cullen, 68; Cape Breton Highlands National Park, 111; Eagle Ridge Inn & Resort, 121, 125, 126, 128, 130, 131, 132, 134, 136; Grand View Lodge, 146, 151, 152, 153, 155; Kohler Co., 164, 169, 170, 174, 175, 176; Randy McCune, Natural Expressions Ltd., 186, 191; Boyne USA Resorts, 190, 196, 200, 201, 202; Leanna Rathkelly, 208, 209, 211, 214, 219, 222; Isobel MacLaurin, 218; The Resort Semiahmoo, 227, 229, 230, 231, 232, 233, 234, 235; Mike Klemme, Golfoto, 228, 232; Dost & Evans, Focus on Golf, 245, 249–50, 252, 257, 258, 260, 266, 271–72; Ed Park, 246, 259, 265; Jay Bowerman, 250, 254, 257, 259, 262, 263; Sunriver Resort, 253; Chriss Szabo, 264; Pebble Beach Company, 270, 274; The Boulders, 310; Kiawah Island Resort, 327, 328; Pinehurst Resort & Country Club, 339, 340, 342, 343, 344, 345–46, 347, 349; Dr. J.H. Carter, 367; The Homestead, 386, 389, 396, 397, 400; Callaway Gardens, 403, 405, 407, 408, 409, 417

Digital Imaging and Production: Louban Media, Regina, Saskatchewan, Canada
A Business of VICOM Multimedia Inc.

Printing: Friesens Corporation, Altona, Manitoba, Canada

Library of Congress Cataloging-in-Publication Data

Stewart, Thomas P.
     The nature of golf: exploring the beauty of the game / Thomas P. Stewart
  and Russell Shoeman.
     p.   cm.
  Includes bibliographical references and index.
  ISBN: 0-9625276-2-9
  LCCN: 98-094031
     1. Golf—Nature.   2. Golf—Photography.   3. Golf—Environment.
  4. Golf—Natural History.   5. Nature—Golf.   6. Nature—Photography.
  7. Photography—Golf.   8. Photography—Nature.   9. Environment—Golf.
  I. Stewart, Thomas P.   II. Title.

For distribution information please call 910-295-9775

The Setting of the Sun
by Jaime DiPietro

As the sun sinks back into endless sky,
I sink too, my heart pulling me lifetimes away,
and I stand again reborn, in our circle
of friendship and love, old memories
making music still today, and echoes of children
laughing and playing, and first best friends.
Amidst innocence we basked, and whispered
and learned and loved everything we could,
and then as we began to fade away, orange fire
smothered by black sky, I bury a piece of my heart
with them, the truest, purest piece.

CONTENTS

ACKNOWLEDGEMENTS

To my immediate family who are so supportive of my endeavors. To Audrey Collins-McMullen for lending me her literary insight and expertise...and especially to my friend Russell Shoeman who allowed me to become his partner in this wonderful project.

Tom Stewart

When I launched this project nearly four years ago I was pretty "green" regarding how much time and effort would be required to bring the work to fruition, which in retrospect may have been a blessing. Not initially understanding the entire process helped me to focus on the day-to-day business of getting the job done, a task that couldn't have been completed without the support, caring and patience of a number of remarkable people, including my mother and father, Joan and Joe; my brothers, Randy and Ray; my daughter, Jennifer; and my friends, Karen Louis, Tom, Ilana and Bryan Stewart, Chriss, Garry and Margaret Szabo, Natalie and Zacki Pere, Katja Izzard, Gloria Shoeman, Ken and Joan Newman, Lynn and Carol Lowes, Louis and Maureen Toth, Janice Hopkins, Dick Wallace, Donna Palamarek, Louis Schinborn, Betty Anne Hopke, Linda White, Doug Coleman, Jonathan Schilling, Bob McDonald, Jodi Tiefenbach, Randi Radcliff, Ruth Schmahl, Derek Barnes, Ken and Shirley Taylor, Mark Glickman, Jack Bickart, Stephen and Barbara Boyd, Patricia Holdsworth, Gene Fryberger, George and Lois Cullen, Brad Cassidy, Jaime DiPietro, Tracy and Shelley Boen, and Jim Shekula. Also, I wish to thank the folks from the various organizations who so diligently assisted us, including Lorne Rubenstein, Brian McCallen, Kathy Prickett, Rachel Crumbley, David Voye, Roxayne Spruance, Dave Zunker, Karen Miller, Karen Oliver, Bob Graunke, Yolanda Butts, George Caldwell, Leza Eckardt, Sue Bombenger, Mark Ronnei, Sue Kuhn, Jackie Clark, Len Reed, Stephen Barba, Tina Chasse, Ed Allmann, Wendy Brinkley, Nancy Magnus, Jeff Hayes, Lee Bowden, Jim Frise, Janelle Griffin, Michele Holder, Penina Freedman, Sonya Hwang, Ashley Truluck, and Beth Doughty.

Russell Shoeman

Throughout my PGA career, many people have considered me as one who especially appreciated beauty in all its forms. I took Walter Hagen's sage advice, which was "to stop and smell the flowers along the way." I have always been pleasantly surprised and richly rewarded by the experience.

As I read through *The Nature of Golf*, it reminds me of how lucky I am to have played the game for so long with such breathtaking beauty as a backdrop. This book will entice every golfer who has a soul. Quite simply, it serves as a personal scrapbook of the reasons why every golfer loves to play the game.

Russell Shoeman is, without a doubt, one of the best and most creative nature photographers in North America. Each new page and every charming image testifies to his love for the game of golf, the people who play it, and the intrinsic splendor of its courses.

Tom Stewart's research and commentary generously depict the geological genesis and illustrate the natural history of the terrain which is our playground. His inspired study has captured the essence of what gives the game its indomitable spirit.

The Nature of Golf is an exhaustive treasury of how well naturalists and sportsmen alike share their common interests in the same landscape. Golfers are, by practice, conservationists. Replacing divots and caring for turf and terrain are obvious, selfless acts of preservation and stewardship. This one-of-a-kind book is a virtual showcase of the harmony between sport, nature and art. Well done boys! And, thanks for being that shining light in the rear-view mirror of our memories.

— *Doug Sanders*

Doug Sanders is an author, adventurer and philanthropist. He has played the PGA Tour for over 40 years and has won over 20 events. He remains one of the great ambassadors for golf all over the world.

WINTERGREEN RESORT

The pastoral setting of the Rockfish Valley gently envelops Wintergreen's Rodes Farm.

When the surveyor's stakes went up at a planned new resort in central Virginia, it was like waving a red flag at biologist Doug Coleman. He knew that this sector of Virginia's Blue Ridge Mountains was a botanist's paradise. More than 500 wildflower species—including a number of rare orchids, lilies, and ferns—had been identified in that very location. Doug would not sit quietly by and allow the bulldozers to scrape away the delicate beauty that had flourished there for eons. Coleman, a teacher at a local community college, decided to do what he does best: educate. He approached Wintergreen Resort's managers to make them aware of the living treasures that were growing under their feet. Once familiar with the site's valuable cache of natural resources, they began to appreciate and cherish the abundance, eventually coming to regard the wilderness as an asset to be diligently protected.

Advancing ecological research and education is an unwavering priority at Wintergreen. In support of this noble ambition, the 11,000-acre resort has set aside more than half of its area as a permanent, undisturbed mountain refuge. The remaining acreage is reserved for such compelling fresh-air pursuits as golf, tennis, swimming, horseback riding, hiking, skiing, fishing, and canoeing.

The combination has been an unqualified success, earning praise and distinctions from the publishers of *Better Homes and Gardens*, *Family Circle*, *Tennis*, *Skiing*, *Golf Digest*, and *Golf Magazine*. In addition, the American Hotel and Motel Association honored Wintergreen Resort's year-round outdoor programming with its "National Environmental Achievement Award."

The surging popularity of ecotourism over the past couple decades has given birth to a related concept known as ecorecreation: mixing regular vacation activities with progressive nature studies. From the outset, the resort and its not-for-profit partner, The Wintergreen Nature Foundation, have been tireless advocates of this ever-changing trend.

2

Autumn's engaging colors dress up the 5th (above) and 8th (below) holes at Devils Knob.

3

Devils Knob #10

Here in the midst of some of the oldest geological formations in North America, one can hike along mountain trails in the morning, attend a naturalist's lecture in the afternoon, and take a golf lesson in the early evening before the sun settles behind the western Blue Ridge range.

Wintergreen's environmental strategies have influenced every aspect of the resort's operation. Prior to breaking ground, a number of property owners talk with consultants so they can learn to be responsible stewards of their land. Caring for the precious flora and fauna is a neighborhood commitment at Wintergreen, even if it means occasionally altering building plans to do so. Many people even volunteer their time and labor to move plants from areas earmarked for clearing.

Flowering dogwoods (above left) and pink azaleas (above right) enrich the perimeters of the 13th hole at Devils Knob (below).

Devils Knob #17

Each year, these merciful undertakings relocate countless indigenous plants to the resort's open spaces and home sites, including plenty of forest species whose populations have existed for thousands of years.

One especially ancient fern bed (discovered by The Wintergreen Nature Foundation staff as they inventoried rare flora) was transplanted to the National Arboretum in Washington, D.C. To reward the resort for its vigilance, Mrs. Lyndon B. Johnson dedicated a wildflower garden at Wintergreen in 1985.

Great laurel (below left) and catawba rhododendrons (below right) thrive within the woods of the closing hole at Devils Knob (above).

7

Some years back, one of Wintergreen's most extraordinary natural gardens was saved from a proposed real estate development. The lush mountain plot supported masses of pink and white trillium blossoms amid tangled groupings of trees, shrubs, and ferns. Because the wooded tract was so adored, the Wintergreen Property Owners Association brought together all concerned parties in an attempt to stave off the excavators.

The 9th at Devils Knob confronts players with one of the course's steepest climbs.

After several meetings, the developers generously offered to leave the acreage untouched if the Property Owners Association reimbursed them for two-thirds of the land's appraised value. Thanks to the overwhelming acceptance of the offer, the Trillium Field continues to astound onlookers with its dazzling springtime displays.

The mountain that now shelters Wintergreen was historically called "Old Appalachia" by geologists. From its 3,800-foot elevation, piedmont hills and valleys can sometimes be seen forty to fifty miles away. When paired with the depths of the Rockfish Valley, this glorious alpine topography makes for some intriguing golf course terrain.

Highlights of Wintergreen's Spring Wildflower Symposium include Doug Coleman's plant identification walks (bottom), Hal Horwitz's macro photography instruction (top), and Jim Troy's medicinal and edible plant talks (center).

9

Wintergreen operates two courses: one roller-coasters abruptly past hardwood forests, rock outcroppings, brooks, and ponds; the other flows easily alongside cornfields, pastures, streams, and glens. Together, the two championship designs are often referred to as "Jekyll and Hyde."

Devils Knob, the highest golf course in Virginia, opened in 1977 after three years of careful planning. Resting entirely on the crest of a mountain, the rigorous layout distracts players with commanding views of the Blue Ridge range and the Shenandoah Valley. Ellis Maples wisely shaped the course to fit the mountain rather than making the mountain fit the course.

Trillium House is a popular haven for woodchucks (below) and rose-breasted grosbeaks (above left and right).

10

The Shamokin Springs Nature Preserve is enhanced by its rocky watercourse (left), unique arrangements of shelf fungi (bottom right), and healthy specimens of goatsbeard (bottom center) and large-flowered trillium (bottom left).

Holes which rise and fall up to 250 feet nurture such impressive Blue Ridge flora as rhododendrons, azaleas, dogwoods, mayapples, lady's slippers, and bloodroot. A sampling of the course's wild inhabitants can be observed in the backyard gardens of the Trillium House, an elegant country inn nestled beside the seventeenth green. Primarily due to its altitude, Devils Knob has a somewhat abbreviated golf season; after that, snow is likely to be the prevailing hazard.

In the Rockfish Valley, however, temperatures range ten to fifteen degrees warmer than on the mountain, keeping Stoney Creek's twenty-seven holes playable all year-long.

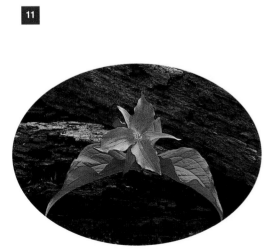

In 1988, the Monocan and Shamokin nines were dramatically mated with the location's racing streams, strapping hills, and primeval forests by architect Rees Jones. Inspiring glimpses of hazy blue mountain peaks are available from practically every teebox, fairway, and putting green.

In the spring of 1998, Stoney Creek's Tuckahoe nine was opened up for Wintergreen's residents and guests. Working closely with environmental agencies, local naturalists, and Tuckahoe's builders, Jones conceived an exquisite test of golf that masterfully struck a balance between a multitude of conflicting requests and regulations. The "eco-friendly" creation features unspoiled wildlife habitats, demanding water hazards, robust elevation changes, and more of Jones's free-form mounds and bunkers.

American goldfinches (above),
delicate spiderworts (below),
and swollen bracket fungi (right)
decorate the Chestnut Springs Trail.

12

13

Fragile clumps of wild geraniums (left) and yellow lady's slippers (far left) lend flashes of color to the rugged profile of the Upper Shamokin Falls (above).

Several sections of The Plunge's trail reveal breathtaking Blue Ridge vistas (above) and jagged pedlar gneiss rock formations (below).

Backed by a tremendous array of activities, Wintergreen Resort and The Wintergreen Nature Foundation have fashioned their home into a highly evolved four-season retreat.

Each May, the Nature Foundation conducts its acclaimed Spring Wildflower Symposium. Noted biologists, photographers, authors, and artists treat participants to first-class workshops, lectures, slide shows, and field trips.

Beneath The Plunge's lower overlook (above), a heavy fog bank silently fills the long valley (below).

Recognizing the importance of getting children excited about their natural surroundings, the resort and the Nature Foundation arrange outings and camps for kids.

The Ravens Roost turnout on the Blue Ridge Parkway serves up panoramic views of neighboring mountain chains.

During the spring and summer, sessions running from a few hours to four or five days initiate kids to the outdoors through such adventures as rock-climbing, rappeling, hiking, canoeing, stream inspections, butterfly walks, and salamander searches.

Mountain laurel (above left) and wild columbine (above right) survive in the thick understories of the Parkway's woods.

Covering nearly thirty miles of wooded mountain and valley terrain, Wintergreen's extensive network of marked hiking trails are constantly maintained for people's enjoyment and education. Staff from the Foundation's Nature Center lead interpretive hikes over these trails, organize special annual events, and advise those wishing to tour the resort on their own. The team of naturalists can even recommend "must see" stops on the legendary Appalachian Trail and Blue Ridge Parkway. Inside the Nature Center, numerous exhibits, books, maps, and gifts help to round out the wilderness experience.

Autumns in central Virginia are simply unforgettable. Programs at Wintergreen celebrating this enchanting time of year include: Virginia's Natural History Retreat Weekend, an annual study of the area's plants, birds, mammals, reptiles, amphibians, rocks, and fossils; and the Fall Foliage Nature Series, which features guided walks into brilliantly hued forests, and chair lift rides up to color-splashed summits.

The Blue Ridge Parkway harbors an amazing variety of fauna, from five-lined skinks (above) to white-tailed deer (below).

Monocan #6

To further serve its members and guests, The Wintergreen Nature Foundation introduced The Field Studies Institute in 1998. Hosted by a select group of naturalists, the weekend get-togethers mix classroom learning with outdoor excursions. Butterfly Identification and Gardening, The Fungus Among Us, Woodland Wildlife, and Trout Stream Ecology are just a few examples of the dynamic new offerings.

Unlike many resorts, Wintergreen doesn't slow down come winter. Its outstanding ski operation boasts a diverse collection of slopes, comprehensive teaching facilities, an award-winning children's program, and a dedicated snowboard terrain park.

With so much winter recreation tailored for people of all ages and abilities, *Skiing* magazine declared Wintergreen to be "the South's single best ski resort."

From the shores of mountain-ringed Lake Monocan (opposite page top), families of wood ducks (below left)
and Canada geese (below right) watch golfers challenge the course's 4th (opposite page bottom) and 5th (above) holes.

The luxurious Wintergarden Spa indulges its patrons with saunas, hot tubs, indoor and outdoor swimming pools, an exercise room, and various other health club amenities.

COURTESY OF JANICE HOPKINS-SNABLY

WINTERGREEN RESORT: CHAPTER 1

Monocan #7

For those who crave more, Wintergreen Resort is a short drive away from a myriad of other attractions within Nelson County—a region famous for its enticing mix of traditional values and contemporary lifestyles.

Crabtree Falls, the highest waterfall east of the Mississippi River, is situated in the county's scenic western corner. The powerful cascade is just one of the many natural wonders which may be explored inside the 1.1 million-acre George Washington National Forest.

Shamokin #2

For leisurely strolls and quiet reflections, the valleys contain an assortment of vineyards, fruit orchards, and picnic parks. Waltons Mountain Museum, located at the birthplace of *The Waltons* creator, Earl Hamner, Jr., is open for fans of the beloved television show.

Caches of spring beauty (opposite page right) and wild bergamot (opposite page left) outline the edges of Shamokin's 6th hole (below).

History buffs will revel in the area's cultural landmarks, which include the homes of three American presidents—James Madison's Montpelier, Thomas Jefferson's Monticello, and James Monroe's Ash Lawn–Highland; Oak Ridge Estate, a Colonial Revival mansion built in 1802; and Woodson's Mill, a water-driven grist mill that has been turning since 1794.

In its mission statement, The Wintergreen Nature Foundation pledges to "encourage the understanding, appreciation, and conservation of the natural resources of the Blue Ridge Mountains of central Virginia." Furthermore, it promises to "function as a research and education facility for its members and visitors, and will serve as a host site for regional and national conservation efforts." Faithful compliance to these lofty goals has established Wintergreen as one of the leaders of the modern environmental movement, a position most other communities are still striving to reach.

Shamokin's par-three 7th hole

Tuckahoe's 3rd hole (above) is home to such fascinating creatures as black vultures (below left) and cottontail rabbits (below right).

Quantities of spring larkspur (below left) and green-and-gold (below right) flowers pattern the fringes of Tuckahoe's 2nd hole (above).

27

Tuckahoe's par-three 4th hole (below) presents players with an expansive marshland and reclusive eastern box turtles (above).

Tuckahoe #9

Stoney Creek's timeless allure is magnified by Nelson County's sweeping pasturelands and Blue Ridge backdrops.

Doug Coleman's Nature Foundation hikes (above) are highlighted by up-close examinations of turk's-cap lilies (above left), long-bracted green orchids (below left), marbled salamanders (opposite page top), and the Lower Shamokin Falls (opposite page bottom).

WINTERGREEN RESORT: CHAPTER 1

Humpback Rocks' restored pioneer mountain farmstead (above) and Nelson County's stately Oak Ridge Estate (below) help to tell the tale of central Virginia's eclectic past.

Evening sunrays fan across the sky above Devils Knob.

AMELIA ISLAND
PLANTATION

The award-winning resort is backdropped by the unspoiled scenery of Amelia Island.

Named after a king's daughter and once home to pirates, Amelia Island lies in the southernmost position of what tourist brochures call the "Golden Isles." With golden sand beaches, golden sunshine, and even the thought of long-buried gold doubloons, the title perfectly describes this string of Atlantic barrier reef islands stretched between North Carolina and Florida.

Among the most golden of these superlative "Golden Isles" is Amelia Island. Its eighteen square miles of sun and sand have been controlled by eight different sovereign nations since 1562; its thirteen-mile-long coast has been named one of the world's ten most beautiful beaches; and its Amelia Island Plantation is perennially chosen as one of the twelve best golf resorts in the United States.

That which glitters here is built upon a history as old as the Ten Commandments. While the people of Israel were crossing the Jordan, Timucua Indians were populating the northeastern corner of the place we now call Florida. The Timucua used stone tools, grew two food crops per year, cultivated tobacco, cooked in clay pots, and ate and lived well on the island they called *Napoyca*—well enough that both men and women attained a height of six to seven feet and enjoyed a life span three times that of most Europeans.

Timucuan society was ideally organized. At its peak, the tribe was directed by a high chief and thirty sub-chiefs—roles which were determined by their mothers' lineage. The chief's skin was etched by sharpened shells to fashion the tattoos which distinguished him from his sub-chiefs.

Their villages consisted of thirty to forty wooden houses covered with reeds and palm fronds; separate domed huts stored meat, vegetables, and animal skins. There was no need to lock up these warehouses; they were left unguarded and kept full for communal use.

The Plantation's spectacular marshlands hug Oysterbay's par-three 3rd (above) and 7th (opposite page) holes.

Tribal ethics alone prevented anyone from taking more than they needed. A large oblong structure at the village's core served as a community center for elders to gather and make collaborative decisions. During council meetings, a few select men were allowed to drink *casina*, a highly caffeinated stimulant. Drunkenness wasn't an issue for these people.

This well-ordered lifestyle was maintained by the Timucua for nearly 3,000 years—until Ponce de León landed in Florida in 1513 and claimed the peninsula for Spain.

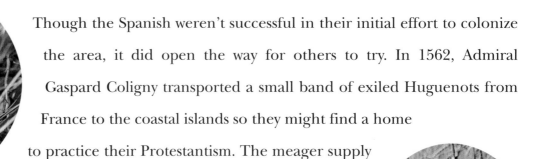

Though the Spanish weren't successful in their initial effort to colonize the area, it did open the way for others to try. In 1562, Admiral Gaspard Coligny transported a small band of exiled Huguenots from France to the coastal islands so they might find a home to practice their Protestantism. The meager supply of food they were left with was traded to the Indians for gold and silver. Not able to adapt to their unfamiliar environment, they desperately set out on the ocean, hoping to return to France. Only cannibalism kept a few men alive long enough to be saved by an English ship.

The sanctuary surrounding Oysterbay's 8th hole (below)
is highlighted by graceful tricolored herons (above right), tree-dwelling raccoons (above left), and flowering seedbox plants (opposite page bottom).

Oceanside #5

Two years later, another French expedition would attempt to settle the islands. Jacques le Moyne, a cartographer who mapped the coastline, rivers, and Indian villages, was one of the voyagers. His work has provided historians with the most complete written record of Timucuan culture.

AMELIA ISLAND PLANTATION: CHAPTER 2

Oakmarsh #5

Choosing a strategic point near the St. John's River, the French commenced building Fort Caroline. Concerned for his people's safety, Saturiba, chief of the Timucua, led hundreds of javelin-carrying tribesmen to the toiling newcomers. Upon seeing the impressive delegation of seven-foot warriors, the French immediately pledged allegiance to the Indians. In their naivete, the Timucua trusted the promise and believed no harm would come from the strangers.

The resurrection ferns covering the hole's oaks (left) shelter broad-headed skinks (below left) and green anoles (below right).

The promise was soon broken. Inept at feeding themselves, the French consumed their year's supply of rations in just one month. They neither cultivated crops nor acquired the Indians' taste for alligator, turtle, or snake.

Oakmarsh #9

Initially they swapped their mirrors, beads, and tools for food, but soon there was nothing left to swap. Hungry and discouraged, they raided the unattended storehouses of the Timucua.

With the coming of winter, life for the French became even bleaker. The Indians migrated further south, leaving the colonists completely on their own. The handful of men who didn't starve to death were eventually rescued by an English slave trader, whose sympathy for them quickly dissolved when he discovered they had done nothing to help themselves, other than to make wine from local grapes.

Still, he fed the survivors and intended to sail them back to Europe. Anticipating their departure, the French destroyed Fort Caroline. Almost as soon as the walls had crashed down, seven French ships arrived with fresh supplies and settlers. The garrison had to be rebuilt.

Boardwalks at Walker's Landing (above left) allow hikers to study great blue herons (above right) and great egrets (right) in their natural habitats.

The self-guided Sunken Forest Trail explores an ancient maritime forest ecosystem.

A richly patterned anhinga (left) dries its wings near the head of Drummond Point's marsh walk (below).

Their good fortune, however, would be short-lived. In 1565, eight Spanish ships moved troops to a camp at St. Augustine, from where they plotted the demise of their French adversaries.

The fates of the French and Indian populations were decided by the cruel Spanish governor, Pedro Menendez de Aviles. He detested the French Protestants and the native "savages" who refused to embrace Christianity. Under his directive, the Spanish soldiers attacked ferociously, sparing only women and children. The next two centuries of Spanish reign was responsible for the slaughter of more than one million people.

The ensuing years continued to be volatile ones for the resilient island, which flew the flag of six different nations between 1763 and 1865. In 1763, the British seized the island from the Spanish and named it Amelia, in honor of King George II's daughter. Twenty years later, the Spanish regained control and founded the island's only town: Fernandina.

The resort's protected shoreline (below) supports an array of island flora and fauna, including beach sunflowers (above left), gopher tortoises (above right), short-billed dowitchers (opposite page top), gaillardias (opposite page bottom left), and butterfly-peas (opposite page bottom right).

ENVIRONMENTALLY SENSITIVE AREA

PLEASE STAY OFF THE DUNES

Its seaport attracted such notorious pirates as Lafitte, Blackbeard, Luis Aury, and Captain Kidd, who made it their headquarters and cache for the golden spoils of their profession.

In 1812, an independent patriot group captured Amelia for one day and presented it to the United States government, which was too busy warring with the British to prevent the Spanish from forcing their way to power one last time.

George MacGregor, a Scottish mercenary, headed the campaign that would finally rid the territory of Spanish tyranny. MacGregor enlisted the help of pirate Luis Aury, who subsequently ruled Amelia himself under the Mexican flag. The little island, named for a princess, became a scarlet woman, a "Wild West town" of bordellos and bars. Dismayed by its unruly reputation, President James Monroe deployed a division of soldiers to claim the location for the United States, which it held until the Civil War. Then in 1861, the Confederate army quietly took Amelia's Fort Clinch, but pulled out early in 1862. In 1868, three years after the end of the war, the beleaguered island was officially annexed to the reunified country.

AMELIA ISLAND PLANTATION: CHAPTER 2

Following the Civil War, Fernandina prospered as a shipping town and Amelia Island became a winter retreat for wealthy Northeast capitalists. Shortly after their grand Victorian mansions were erected, fortunes were reversed

by the Great Depression. Railroads replaced shipping, but Amelia Island survived on the strength of its fledgling shrimping operations (which presently account for 80 percent of Florida's Atlantic white shrimp catch).

The boggy edges of Long Point's 2nd hole (below) accommodate white ibis (above left) and yellow-crowned night-herons (above right).

Tangled live oaks and matted dune grasses frame Long Point's 6th green.

As the world's environmental conscience began to emerge, the popularity of nature-based destinations flourished. In 1970, Charles Fraser purchased a wild, overgrown piece of the island from Union Carbide. The mining company had intended to tear up the site, but Fraser had much kinder plans for the 1,300 acres.

Today, Amelia Island Plantation is one of Florida's greenest parks. Its bracing wetlands, beaches, sand dunes, and coastal forests are all "thoughtfully developed—and undeveloped."

The 16th hole at Long Point (above) provides a low wetland habitat for such moisture-loving plants as golden-clubs (opposite page right) and purple gerardias (opposite page left).

When Charles Fraser needed a designer for the resort's first golf course, he invited Pete Dye to take on the demanding assignment. Respecting the natural lay of the land, Dye gently carved twenty-seven holes of golf into the glorious subtropical terrain. In 1972, his Amelia Links was ready for the Plantation's golfers.

Oakmarsh is the longest and toughest nine at Amelia Links. The narrow holes are ruggedly defended by the island's twisted live oaks, arrow-straight pines, writhing tidal creeks, and sweeping marshlands; clusters of well-placed fairway and greenside bunkers complete the challenge.

With four of its holes built on the brink of a vast salt marsh, Oysterbay is widely regarded as the most scenic of the three courses. To steer clear of the formidable hazard, players usually find that precision will serve them better than power.

As its name implies, the Oceanside nine does reach the beach. The course's fourth through sixth holes are tightly squeezed between the Plantation's towering sand dunes and sparkling seashore. Forty-foot-high dunes are covered with the plants which help to hold their massive forms, and the signs which help to remind people to stay off their fragile surfaces.

In 1987, Tom Fazio finished the Long Point Club. Like Dye, Fazio integrated the best of the island's existing features into his magnificent design. To showcase Long Point's crescent-shaped coastline, maritime forests, and vigorous marshlands, Fazio painstakingly arranged the holes over the location's primeval ribbons of high ground (ground that was raised up eons ago as the sea receded at the end of the last Ice Age). Broad, shimmering views of Nassau Sound and the Atlantic Ocean combine to make the experience even more memorable.

Long Point #17

A number of years back, the resort's most precious natural resource was in jeopardy. Because its beaches were gradually disintegrating, the South Amelia Island Shore Stabilization Association raised $6.6 million to move more than 2,000 cubic yards of sand from an offshore "borrow pit." The project, completed in only sixty days, buffered the sand dunes, golf holes, and oceanfront infrastructure from the punishing northeast winds and waves which affect the island in the fall and winter. The beach, now nine feet above sea level, was designated a coastal renourishment zone.

On the Plantation's leeward side, coquina trails and cypress board-walks offer easy, low-impact access to the resort's breathtaking wilderness preserves. The maze of footpaths weave through moss-draped oak groves; tour the margins of tremendous salt marshes; and even stretch directly out into the brackish water.

Fernandina's historic Williams House (above) and Palace Saloon (below)

The town's Nassau County Courthouse at night

Even as residential lots are sold at Amelia Island Plantation, its administrators work to save as much of the native landscape as possible. An architectural review board oversees these objectives, assisting with the construction plans of homes so they might be carefully blended into Amelia's pristine surroundings.

Amelia Island Plantation has twice been chosen as the "Best Beach Resort of the Year" by the readers of *Family Circle* magazine. The property has earned these honors with offerings such as children's recreational and educational programs; a five-star tennis and health and fitness center; jogging, walking, and bicycle paths; lagoon, ocean, and freshwater fishing; horseback riding; swimming; and, of course, golf.

Fernandina Harbor teems with local industry and wildlife:
brown pelicans (opposite page bottom), snowy egrets (above), and white pelicans (top) search the shrimp boat docks (below) for an easy meal.

Fort Clinch (above and below) has stood guard on Amelia Island's northern shore since the mid-nineteenth century.

Legends persist that its colorful past has left Amelia Island riddled with ghosts. Headless Confederate soldiers are occasionally sighted at Fort Clinch, and the reflections of long-dead bartenders can sometimes be seen in the Palace Saloon's mirror—or so it is said. It's hard to deny, however, that Amelia does possess a rare ability to beckon back anyone who has ever sampled her irresistible charms.

Sunset glows across Oakmarsh's placid tidal creek.

THE *Balsams* GRAND RESORT HOTEL

Nestled between Lake Gloriette and New Hampshire's White Mountains, the cherished hotel has been welcoming guests for more than a century.

A pint of locally prepared maple syrup awaits return visitors in their guest rooms at The BALSAMS Grand Resort Hotel in Dixville Notch, a tiny community in northern New Hampshire's White Mountains.

Fall is considered a peak season here. Vibrant autumn colors reflect from maple, birch, poplar, and ash, contrasting against the dark spruce, pine, balsam, and cedar which thrive in the cool upper altitudes.

Trees and tourism are critical to the New Hampshire economy, so it is satisfying, if not unusual, to learn that The BALSAMS has successfully combined the two industries. The resort's priceless natural resources are shrewdly managed so that it can function both as a certified tree farm and as a four-season, four-star, and four-diamond hotel. Its 15,000 pristine acres are open to the public approximately forty weeks of each year.

At The BALSAMS, winter brings alpine skiing and snowboarding on award-winning slopes, cross-country skiing along fifty miles of trails, snowmobiling, ice-skating, and snowshoeing. Summer ushers in swimming, fishing, hiking, golf, boating, lawn sports, and tennis. Camp Wind Whistle entertains youngsters with guided nature walks, numerous indoor and outdoor games, and a variety of arts and crafts projects.

Responsibly utilizing and preserving wilderness areas are two primary missions of the resort's recreational, educational, and operational programs here in this narrow granite gorge. Besides providing humans and wildlife with valuable living space, the resort's timber harvesting and watershed protection practices also work hand in hand to minimize soil erosion, forest fires, and tree diseases.

On an even more obvious level, wood waste from tree farm forestry operations (up to fifty-eight tons per day) is used to supplement the resort's energy needs. A steam and electricity co-generation plant saves the burning of up to 200,000 gallons of fossil fuels per month, or a million gallons per year.

Early morning fog lingers in the valley below The PANORAMA's 9th hole.

The original hotel was a quaint New England rest stop known as the Dix House when it opened in 1866. As its reputation spread, it was repeatedly expanded and upgraded but continued to be called the Dix House until Henry S. Hale acquired the property and renamed it The BALSAMS in 1896.

Hale needed food for his patrons, so he bought up neighboring land and leased it to farmers who grew produce and raised meat for the hotel. He soon realized that people wanted more than a meal and a place to sleep, so he built Lake Gloriette for boating and angling enthusiasts. Then in 1897, he authorized the construction of a modest little six-hole golf course.

Modern amenities were slow to climb the mountains until the resort's state-of-the-art hydro-electric plant was completed. Mud Pond and its reservoir and canal system collected and carried water down from the mountain to the hotel and its surrounding farms. With so many comforts and conveniences available in such a remote place, The BALSAMS flourished.

The PANORAMA #6

In 1912, Donald Ross routed eighteen new golf holes to replace the old six-hole course. Set into the heaving slopes of Keyser Mountain, Ross's strapping creation is one of New England's finest examples of a scenic, yet challenging layout. Located just two miles from the hotel, The PANORAMA provides players with breathtaking views of adjoining mountain chains, and occasional glimpses of eagles, ospreys, herons, moose, and bear.

The PANORAMA's formidable 13th hole tumbles down Keyser Mountain's west face.

The PANORAMA #4

With the new golf course, The BALSAMS reinforced its standing as a trendsetter amongst Northeast resorts. In fact, New Hampshire's first multi-storey fireproof structure was built here: a steel and concrete design reminiscent of castles along the Rhine. Indeed, anyone who wanted to be treated royally came to The BALSAMS for such well-heeled pastimes as riding, polo, and skeet shooting.

The course's timberlands shelter and feed local black bears. COURTESY OF THE BALSAMS

After World War II, however, the nation's vacation habits took a sharp turn and destination resorts lost favor with travelers. By the mid-50s, The BALSAMS was bankrupt.

Boston businessman Neil Tillotson had ancestral roots in the county, and when the hotel came up for sale, he bought it. Years before, Tillotson had started up a prosperous manufacturing company after discovering an economical way to mass produce latex goods such as balloons and medical gloves. When he purchased The BALSAMS, his plan was to relocate the Tillotson Corporation headquarters to the hotel complex, an ingenious strategy to reduce operating expenses for both entities.

The par-three 7th hole (below) is gently backdropped by the rolling hills of Quebec, Canada's "La Belle Province."

To manage the property, Tillotson chose four men who had been employees of The BALSAMS: a former caddy, ski instructor, chef, and construction crew supervisor. Together, their remarkable vision and determination put the business back in the black without missing a season. Today, about eight out of every ten registered guests are returning friends of The BALSAMS.

The PANORAMA's forests are enriched by delicate woodland sunflowers (opposite page top), hardy Jack-in-the-pulpits (above left), and vigorous hobblebush plants (above).

The secret of its enduring appeal is threefold: a carefully tended alpine setting in which to enjoy an endless number of activities; a restoration, renovation, and redecoration effort that polished up the hotel's romantic Old World charm; and impeccably trained service staff—who actually outnumber the 400-guest capacity of the resort!

The unspoiled mountain and valley environments which envelop The BALSAMS are interpreted for visitors by a full-time naturalist and support staff who lead year-round hikes over an impressive network of marked trails.

The 12th green (above) rests high above the wetlands which function as rookeries for The PANORAMA's mallard ducks (below).

To further delight its guests, the resort actively participates in the New Hampshire Wildlife Viewing Program. Established by the New Hampshire Fish and Game Department, this program focuses on two species in particular: moose and the endangered peregrine falcon. Observation areas are maintained so people can quietly study these creatures in their native habitats.

An assortment of plant and animal guide books are available for those who wish to explore the wilderness on their own. A perceptive hiker may come across mink, fox, snowshoe hares, porcupines, raccoons, muskrats, beavers, coyotes, and fishers.

Birders may sight red-tailed hawks, northern three-toed woodpeckers, cliff swallows, and ruby-throated hummingbirds. For people with a passion for entomology, the mountain is home to spectacular populations of mourning cloak and white admiral butterflies.

Showy blue (above left) and yellow flag (above right) irises edge the marsh alongside the 4th green (below).

Perched above Lake Gloriette, the historic Grand Resort Hotel (above) offers up commanding views of Dixville Notch (below).

Wildflower lovers are presented with such treasured species as blue flag iris, pink lady's slipper, and painted trillium. Mountain cranberry and Iceland and reindeer mosses are found at higher elevations; and in a few rocky zones containing unusually high concentrations of lime, Dutchman's breeches have even been known to bloom.

Raccoons (below), tree swallows (above left), and ruby-throated hummingbirds (above right) are a few of the resort's more familiar wild residents.

Mud Pond (above) and Moose Brook (below) lie secluded within the resort's sprawling nature preserve.

Early in its history, a few guests would journey to the resort to pursue their interests in biology and botany.

A young bull moose feeds in the mucky shallows (above) of Two Towns Pond (top).

Some even contributed scientific knowledge about indigenous flora: Robbins' ragwort is a marsh plant of the region named for James Watson Robbins, a gentleman who spent several summers researching the White Mountains' fertile ecology.

Many of the routes that wind through the county were originally worn by the feet of the first inhabitants some 11,000 years ago. Over the centuries, those who followed the Indians found the rugged landscape a difficult one from which to wring a living.

Outings with staff from The BALSAMS Nature Center are highlighted by exhilarating climbs to the Sanguinary Ridge (top) and Table Rock (above) overlooks.

Positioned within Dixville Notch State Park, Huntington's Cascade follows an erratic course down the Notch's jagged south slope.

Their need or greed led them to indiscriminately log the forests,

drain the wetlands, and overcultivate the thin topsoil.

*Foxglove (left) and purple trillium (above)
color the park's woods.*

THE BALSAMS GRAND RESORT HOTEL: CHAPTER 3

South of The BALSAMS, pure mountain water pours down the Baby Flume's terraced canyon.

Now that we realize our roads were once footpaths, we are able to appreciate the wisdom of the native people, whose stride made a softer impact on the Earth, and whose existence did not depend on depleting the sources of life.

What supports the economy today are exquisite meals laid out in view of legendary mountain ranges, elegantly appointed rooms which look out over lush garden plots, and levels of service that go beyond professionalism to genuine concern.

Beyond its standard of hospitality, what spells success for The BALSAMS are little things such as dealing with insect pests in ways that leave the birds unharmed. These examples of enlightened stewardship stem from an underlying respect for the natural world. With that respect as the foundation, development can sing in harmony with the environment, achieving a balance that is sustainable and healthy for both.

The Flume Brook Trail embraces some of North America's most precious wildflowers, including pink (right) and white-form pink lady's slippers (far right).

Beaver Brook Falls, another beloved northern New Hampshire landmark, is located between The BALSAMS and the town of Colebrook.

The BALSAMS' Lake Abeniki mirrors the late evening sky.

THE EQUINOX

The gleaming Equinox Hotel has displayed its New England sophistication for well over two centuries.

A stunning combination of national and natural histories converge in Manchester Village, Vermont's renowned Green Mountain retreat. The Green Mountain Boys met here to plot strategy for their war of independence. Mary Todd Lincoln came here to escape the horrors of the Civil War. But before there were nations and wars, there were simply mountains of limestone and granite covered by vast, impenetrable forests.

Originally populated by the Algonquin, Iroquois, and Abnaki Indians, the location now known as Vermont was secured for France in 1609, when explorer Samuel de Champlain sailed the lake that now bears his name. Upon seeing the mountains which form the spine of the region, the French called them *monts verts* (green mountains), the phrase that was ultimately rearranged to serve as the state's title.

In 1763, the Treaty of Paris officially ended the French and Indian War and granted control of the area to the English. Locally, both New Hampshire and New York claimed the resource-rich land as their own. By 1777, Ethan Allen and his Green Mountain Boys had won their campaign to make the territory a self-governing republic, which it remained until 1791, when Vermont became the fourteenth state in the Union.

Manchester Village's reputation as a seat of hospitality, however, was established long before 1791. In 1769, Marsh Tavern opened its doors and quickly became a popular inn for men to gather and debate their allegiance to the crown or the new colonies. William Marsh, the tavern owner, took sides with the British. His patrons, who sided with the independence movement, chose to seize Marsh's business in the name of their cause. With that, Marsh Tavern became the first Tory property to be commandeered for the revolutionary war effort.

While Vermont sings with the memories of America's earliest military gains, modern attempts to preserve its natural resources are making their own gains.

Vermont's storied autumn colors envelop Gleneagles' 13th (above) and 12th (opposite page) holes.

It has taken a number of decades for the nation to recover from the waves of reckless proprietary harvesting which occurred during an era when the Earth's plants, animals, and minerals were thought to be inexhaustible.

Today, a more conscientious generation strives to maintain the endangered environments which can only survive where undisturbed biodiversity exists.

As one of the state's most precious assets, the Green Mountains are the focus of several cooperative ventures proposing carefully monitored use of designated areas to protect the fragile life found there.

*The woods enclosing the 16th green (above) are beautifully adorned
by collections of bunchberries (below), mushrooms (opposite page left), and shelf fungi (opposite page right).*

The Vermont Land Trust and the Equinox Preservation Trust work together to safeguard extensive tracts of pristine woodlands.

The Nature Conservancy watches over alpine habitats which support unique plant communities, concentrating on two crucial twenty-five-acre parcels that are utilized for sustainability studies. Bennington College and the Burr and Burton Seminary participate in teachings and examinations of the mountains' flora, amphibians, and mammals; and the Vermont Institute of Natural Science is active in ecological research and avian rehabilitation. Sensitive ecosystems on Mount Equinox are now buffered by hundreds of acres of conservation easements regulated by the Vermont Land Trust and The Nature Conservancy.

Perhaps the most curious partner in these endeavors is The Equinox, a remarkably enlightened 1,100-acre golf resort. Resorts are often perceived as the enemy: greedy developers of remote, unspoiled places. In Manchester Village, however, it was the Equinox Resort Associates who created the Equinox Preservation Trust to encourage responsible land use ethics. In addition, the resort's Gleneagles Golf Course was one of the first golf facilities in the country to be registered as a Cooperative Sanctuary by the Audubon Society.

Mountains, while symbols of everlasting strength, can be devastated by too much human intrusion and encroachment.

To help ward off potentially harmful activities, three exceptional zones on Mount Equinox receive exceptional attention. Deer Knoll and Table Rock are two rare openings in the limestone that provides perfect growing conditions for the very rare Richardson's sedge and scirpus-like sedge. The third zone, Cook's Hollow, is one of the Green Mountains' last remaining wild gardens for roseroot stonecrop and smooth woodsia.

Bracing views of Vermont's Green Mountains are revealed from the high hilltops of the 9th (opposite page) and 15th (above) holes.

Hikes through these sectors are led by naturalists from the Vermont Institute of Natural Science. While public access is limited, the locations are visible from special observation stations and picnic grounds.

A few years back, a beloved little spring-fed reservoir at the foot of Mount Equinox was the scene of an intensive rescue effort. Equinox Pond had filled in with centuries of sedimentation, and its springs were being choked off. Excavation crews painstakingly dug out the ten-acre basin by hand, and then edged sections with a wooden walkway to help slow perimeter erosion. Thanks to the diligence of its rescuers, the clear, sparkling pool continues to draw thousands of sightseers each and every year.

Mount Equinox, the inspiring landmark of this rustic corner of New England, has been silent witness to the resort's evolution over the last 230 years. Under the directive of several owners, seventeen major remodelings—representing six distinct architectural styles—succeeded one another on the original Marsh Tavern site.

Gleneagles' finishing hole sweeps gently over the resort's pastoral valley floor.

One of the better known owners was Charles F. Orvis, who acquired the quaint inn next to the main hotel in 1883. A gentleman of tremendous charisma and vision, his tireless promotional work conveyed Manchester's virtues to a broader international clientele.

The family name, now synonymous with quality fly-fishing gear, was at that time closely associated with this upscale destination resort in the Green Mountains. Orvis and his wife organized and hosted dances, concerts, dinners, firework displays, theatrical performances, and various other events which brought villagers and visitors together.

Adjacent to the course, The British School of Falconry's Chris Davis teaches Donna Palamarek the proper handling of a Harris' hawk.

*Robert Todd Lincoln's Hildene (above), Manchester's tree-lined sidewalks (below left),
and the First Congressional Church (below right) are gracious reminders of the area's rich past.*

Literary figures such as Robert Frost, Walter Hard, and Sarah Cleghorn were regular patrons and often read their poetry and prose to fellow sojourners.

However, economic ups and downs took their toll and in 1972, the rickety Equinox Hotel was closed after being declared unsound.

Because it was listed on the National Register of Historic Places, the building was not demolished. Vacant for more than a decade, the property was reopened in 1985 following a $20 million makeover that revived much of its former country manor elegance.

In 1991, The Galesi Group, Guinness Enterprise Holdings (Vermont), Inc., and Callaghan & Partners, Ltd. united to effect further renovations. Teams of architects, engineers, artisans, and laborers worked double shifts to redo the hotel's interior in just three months.

Also in 1991, Rees Jones was brought in to modernize the Equinox Links Club, the resort's sixty-five-year-old Walter Travis design. Jones, a master restorer of classic American golf courses, dramatically reinforced the layout's defenses by setting teeboxes back and repositioning fairway bunkers.

The Equinox Preservation Trust encompasses trickling brooks (below) and quiet, wooded hiking trails (right).

A lone wood duck (below) glides peacefully through the waters of Equinox Pond (above).

Putting surfaces and greenside bunkers were then updated, and when the new irrigation and drainage systems were operational, the resort's showpiece was rededicated as the Gleneagles Golf Course.

An eastern chipmunk (top)
and a black-phase gray squirrel (above) forage along the pond's edge.

Today, The Equinox is acknowledged as a *Golf Magazine* Silver Medal Resort, and its championship golf club is recognized as a shining example of how environmental concerns can be placed on par with design considerations.

Golf, however, is not the only game in town. The Equinox, its concierges, and the neighboring counties can entertain visitors all year-round.

The world renowned Orvis Fly-Fishing School offers instruction in casting techniques, fly tying, rod building, entomology, and stream reading. The American Museum of Fly-Fishing is a popular attraction as is the Battenkill River, a highly regarded trout stream. Hildene, Robert Todd Lincoln's summer estate, accommodates tours, symphony concerts, comedy festivals, craft fairs, and antique shows. A number of local theaters stage musical recitals and off-Broadway productions.

Outdoor pursuits range from tennis, hiking, canoeing, falconry, and hunting to skeet shooting, mountain biking, and horseback riding. Guests of The Equinox may also take advantage of such indoor amenities as a swimming pool and a health and fitness center.

The Trust's upper trails are highlighted by
craggy rock outcroppings (above) and rousing valley overlooks (below).

Close by are a myriad of other attractions, including: the Norman Rockwell Exhibition in Arlington; the Grandma Moses Gallery in Bennington; Bennington Museum; the New England Maple Museum in Pittsford; the Guild of Old-time Crafts and Industries in Weston; and the Green Mountain Flyer, a restored diesel that takes passengers on a twenty-six-mile excursion through the Vermont countryside.

Autumn in New England is nothing short of spectacular. The mountains cradling idyllic Manchester Village radiate each October in brilliant hues of red, yellow, and orange. The valley's unhurried pace and breathtaking landscapes have thrilled generations of "leaf-peepers."

Rolling pastures (above) and covered bridges (right) enhance the scenery of adjoining counties.

The Equinox is equally magnificent when winter insulates the Green Mountains with a coat of white. Twenty-five miles of groomed trails invite cross-country skiers to explore Equinox Pond, the base of Mount Equinox, and

the golf course's hilly terrain. For those craving more vigorous challenges, world-class downhill skiing is featured nearby at Bromley and Stratton Mountains.

Revitalized as a charming, white-columned New England country house, The Equinox embodies Vermont's independent spirit. It has hosted presidents Coolidge, Theodore Roosevelt, Grant, Taft, and Eisenhower while reminding them of their place in history with the slogan, "Serving the Republic since before there was a Republic."

A common goldeneye (top left) and a blue-winged teal (top right) find refuge along the banks of the Battenkill River (above).

Daylight silently fades from the clustered peaks of Vermont's Green Mountains.

HIGHLANDS LINKS/
KELTIC LODGE

The sheltered inlet at Cape Breton's Neil's Harbour bustles with the vitality of its fishing industry.

The ridges and swales, moss-covered forests, and stony trout brook at Highlands Links stretch nearly seven miles from its first tee to its eighteenth green. However, many still choose to go the distance on foot. The walk is tiring, but the delightful sense of accomplishment can more than make up for the lack of mechanized transportation.

The Links are part of Cape Breton Highlands National Park, which encompasses 370 square miles of wild country. Playing a game of golf here is, quite literally, like taking your clubs out on a nature hike. Within the park, 95 percent of which is free from development, visitors can tour some of the oldest rock formations in Atlantic Canada; feel the force of restless ocean winds; smell the perfume of spruce and balsam in the air; watch seals and porpoises swim in the high tidal waters off the coast; and share a view of the Gulf of St. Lawrence with a grazing moose.

"The wilderness waits—" wrote David Olesen in a 1981 issue of *Boundary Waters Canoe Area News*, "a reservoir of silence and darkness held for safekeeping in a world of noise and street lights. It is a gift to the few who live along its edge, and to many who do not. Perhaps most importantly, it is a gift held in trust for those whose lives have not yet begun."

The citizens of Cape Breton long ago recognized the raw, untamed character of their home as a treasure worth preserving. In the early part of the twentieth century, they began to petition the government to set aside an area as a sanctuary. Twenty-two years later, in 1936, the northern tip of the 115-mile-long island was designated a national park to "ensure the long-term perpetuation" of its natural resources.

Thanks to their far-sightedness, Cape Breton Highlands National Park remains a wild place. It's also a place where people can come to experience their kinship with whales and eagles, and to discover tiny descendants of glacial plant life. In fact, the park is one of North America's best maritime locations for finding rare arctic-alpine flora.

Named the fourth most beautiful island in the world by *Condé Nast Traveler* magazine, Cape Breton inspires with the lingering mystery of tranquil, misty valleys; the vibrant melodies of innocent, pastoral hills; and the majestic power of a land that existed before remembering began.

Breathtaking ocean vistas enhance the 4th hole at Highlands Links.

Highlands Links #3

Cape Breton and the deep, narrow Strait of Canso (the channel that separates the island from Nova Scotia's mainland) were formed by the same catastrophic events which uplifted the Appalachian Mountains.

Highlands Links #8

But while the Appalachians have softened and mellowed from the influences of a longer growing season, the north has maintained a primitive ruggedness.

Life is not found here in teeming abundance; fierce waves and winds, frigid ocean currents, and extreme ice scouring prevent all but the hardiest species from gaining a foothold.

The glaciers retreated from this primeval landscape only 10,000 years ago. Their impact: the elevation shifts and bedrock profiles which are responsible for the park's many distinct microclimates and ecosystems. The highland plateau, for instance, at 1,700 feet above sea level, is the tallest point in Nova Scotia. There is more fog, snow, rain, and temperature variance here than on any other part of the island.

Starflowers (above left) and bluebead lilies (above right) pattern the par-three 10th hole's woods (below).

As might be expected, this habitat supports little vegetation. The plateau is boggy and barren, home to stubborn plants stunted from their exposure to the elements: black spruce,
blueberry, dwarf balsam fir, sheep laurel, and reindeer lichen being common examples.

The 15th hole and St Peter's Parish

Franey Mountain and the steeples of St Peter's Parish backdrop the imposing 16th hole.

Boreal forests of primarily balsam fir and black spruce cover approximately half of the park's acreage. The lower sectors, known as the Acadian Land Region, grow fir, spruce, pine, white birch, red maple, beech, and even lush carpets of wildflowers which bloom only after winter releases the island from its icy grip—often not until mid-June. Some of Eastern Canada's oldest hardwood stands flourish here at the northernmost fringes of their range. Twenty-seven different hiking trails showcase this timeless scenery, tracing routes that were first trodden approximately 1,000 years ago.

The tale of Cape Breton's past has been enriched by a number of resourceful cultures. By A.D.1000, Micmac Indians were living along the island's pristine coastline and interior waterways.

The 9th green lies hidden just below the crest of a steep, wooded hilltop.

For hundreds of years, the natives caught the area's whales, brook trout, cod, mackerel, lobsters, snow crabs, and the now endangered Atlantic salmon.

River otters (above left) and great blue herons (above right) fish along the banks of the course's Clyburn Brook (below).

The 13th hole (above) and its resident red fox (below)

The Micmacs took only what they needed to survive, but those who came later weren't nearly as discreet. Commercial fishermen from England, France, Spain, and Portugal crowded and quickly over-exploited Cape Breton's fisheries. As these critical food reserves waned, life became increasingly more difficult for all peoples.

Some historians believe that the English, French, Spanish, and Portuguese weren't the first visitors from the Old World to reach Cape Breton.

The par-three 17th hole

Sheep laurel (below left) and bunchberry (below right) thrive within the dense understories of the 18th hole (above).

Norse mariners are thought to have explored these shores during the tenth century. About five centuries later, in 1497, John Cabot (the Italian-born navigator sailing under the English flag) rediscovered the island. In 1713, the Treaty of Utrecht officially transferred the territory that is now Nova Scotia to the English, finally ending their long, bitter dispute with the French regarding sovereignty of the region.

Hikes around Middle Head are highlighted by unobstructed views of Ingonish Island.

With the arrival of peace, greater numbers of Scottish immigrants set sail for Cape Breton Island, looking to carve out a brand new existence in the "Brave New World".

Freshwater Lake and Cape Smokey

Alexander Graham Bell, renowned inventor of the telephone, was one of those Scot transplants. Born in Edinburgh in 1847, Bell first toured the island when he was thirty-eight years old. So drawn was he to life in the cool northern countryside, that he returned a year later to establish a vacation home in Baddeck. His summer estate, *Beinn Bhreagh* (beautiful mountain), became an important center for the research that would bring welcome prosperity to the remote little island. His scientific endeavors—proudly commemorated at Cape Breton's Alexander Graham Bell National Historic Site—employed hundreds of local laborers and technicians.

Set back from Middle Head's sheer cliffs (above),
the enchanting Keltic Lodge (below) typifies gracious Maritime hospitality.

Dark skies and choppy seas along Cape Breton's windswept eastern banks

Black Brook Beach

Near the turn of the century, Bell invited a friend, Ohio industrialist H.C. Corson, to stay at Beinn Bhreagh. Instantly captivated by Cape Breton's magnificent beauty, Corson purchased the island's Middle Head peninsula in 1904 and built a summer estate of his own.

In 1938, the province of Nova Scotia acquired the peninsula from Corson's widow and annexed it to the national park. To accommodate travelers, small cottages were erected and the former Corson manor was renovated. When the park's golf course was ready for play in 1941, the estate's barn was moved and remodeled to function as a pro-shop and lounge.

Still Brook tumbles into the sea at Black Brook Beach.

Dave Algar utilizes the Broad Cove Outdoor Theatre to entertain his audience with stories of Cape Breton's early settlers.

111

The mucky edges of Warren Lake (above) nourish
healthy populations of moose (below right) and northern pitcher plants (below left).

At the close of World War II, a boom in tourism touched off a demand for additional lodging. Welsford West, the provincial architect, was appointed to draw up plans for an elegant new hotel.

West combined his love of Maritime traditions with his studies of northern European architecture to prepare a blueprint that embraced both Atlantic coast and Swiss alpine design elements. His Keltic Lodge was completed in 1951.

113

The footpath to Mary Ann Falls (above right) is fringed by flocks of noisy ravens (top left) and clumps of false Solomon's seal (above left).

The bluffs and lighthouse at Neil's Harbour

In 1932, four years before the birth of Cape Breton Highlands National Park, Cabot Trail was opened to automobile traffic. Engineered around much of the island's rugged perimeter, the twisting roadway provides sightseers with an exhilarating array of ocean and alpine turnouts and overlooks.

The northern sections of Cabot Trail present commanding views of White Point's idyllic harbour (above) and cove (below).

Lone Shieling, one of the trail's busier stops, is tucked into a mature sugar maple forest near Pleasant Bay and the Grande Anse River. Featuring masonry walls, a thatched roof, and an oversized hearth, the rustic hut is typical of shelters used by Scot shepherds.

Stanley Thompson, a prominent Scottish-born Canadian designer, was commissioned to lay out the park's golf course. Utilizing only crews of men and their horse-drawn machinery, Thompson produced a stunning tribute to Scotland's legendary seaside courses. Each hole at Highlands Links was even identified with a descriptive Gaelic name: *Sair Fecht* (hard work), *Cuddy's Lugs* (donkey's ears), *Tattie Bogle* (potato pits), and *Heich O'Fash* (heap of trouble) being more amusing examples.

In addition to golf, Cape Breton Highlands National Park is set up for a variety of other uses. Specific areas are maintained for administrative services, interpretive exercises, general outdoor recreation, and such low-density activities as backpacking and primitive camping. Park staff carefully watch over habitats which sustain rare or unique flora—in some zones access is strictly prohibited.

Clear mountain water cascades down Beulach Ban Falls.

The wooded trail encircling Lone Shieling (above) exhibits arrangements of shelf fungi (below left) and rosy twisted-stalk (below right).

They are also charged with the enormous responsibilities of preserving and protecting the park's significant cultural relics and vital ecological processes.

Supporting the park's original mission, educators continue to help visitors enjoy and appreciate Cape Breton's celebrated natural resources, from its sea-washed shores to its craggy headlands and vast, open barrens.

Sunset over the Gulf of St. Lawrence

HIGHLANDS LINKS/KELTIC LODGE: CHAPTER 5

ℰAGLE RIDGE
INN & RESORT

Picturesque Lake Galena hosts a wide range of the resort's popular outdoor activities.

The romance of the Mississippi River, the history of the Civil War, the nineteenth-century treasures of architecture, and the soft, scenic beauty of rolling farm country make Galena, Illinois, the rare setting that has everything.

Originally, it was called *manitoomie*, or "God's Country," by the Winnebago Indians, who are thought to be the first humans to inhabit this northwestern corner of the state. In 1827, the region was named Jo Daviess County after a prominent Virginia–Kentucky politician. The name Galena (meaning sulfide of lead) was chosen for the town in 1826.

Three years later, people from all over the world congregated at Galena to participate in the nation's first mineral rush. The vast lead deposits had been mined by the Sac and Fox Indians centuries earlier, but it wasn't until the French arrived in the late 1600s that the taking of metal from the Earth became an enterprise for financial gain. In 1807, the Upper Mississippi Lead Mine District was formed, and Galena was well on its way to becoming the area's busiest river port.

The smelting industry joined hands with the mining industry on land, and the steamboats conducted their commerce on the water, transporting the stuff of Galena's mineral and agricultural operations to hungry markets downriver.

The Winnebago no doubt resented the air that stung their noses, the ungodly sounds which filled their ears, and the encroaching civilization that pushed their game further and further away. These factors led to an uprising in 1830, followed by the Black Hawk War in 1832. To guard the thriving little town, the United States government transformed Galena into a military camp; from this show of strength, a treaty was hastily drawn up, and no major battle took place.

North Course #7

A breathtaking drop and spectacular bunkering define the challenge of the North's par-three 8th hole.

With their newly found wealth and the assurance of peace, the people of Galena began to put down roots. They built luxurious homes on the steep, glacier-carved hills of the town, and then constructed long wooden staircases to help them complete the arduous climb.

Evidence of the area's farming heritage rests alongside the North Course's 11th green.

Stories of Galena's affluence spread. Irish troops, impressed into the British Army and sent to Canada, learned of Illinois' feverish mining activity from the French. Stirred by the prospect of striking it rich, they deserted the British and crossed from Canada to the United States.

One of those Irish expatriates was John Furlong. Upon discovering a sizeable vein of ore just six miles from Galena, he and his partners established the Vinegar Hill Lead Mine. The men did indeed strike it rich, but not without years of back-breaking labor and plenty of gritty determination. Its days of productivity long over, this geological wonder (now owned by Furlong's descendants) is the only lead mine in Illinois open for tours.

Prosperity abounded through the years of the Civil War, when Galena achieved another claim to glory: nine of its citizens served as generals in the Union army. The roster of distinguished soldiers included a future American president, Ulysses S. Grant; a lawyer, John Rawlins; friends of Grant's, John C. Smith and William Rowley; a Consul General to Belgium, Augustus Chetlain; the inventor of the telescopic sight, Jasper Maltby; and a full-blooded Six Nations Seneca warrior, Ely Parker.

Killdeer (above) and wild turkeys (below) search the hole's perimeters for a midday meal.

Nodding trillium (below), hoary vervain (opposite page bottom), and Dutchman's breeches (opposite page top) flourish in the lush woods of the North's 16th hole (above).

After the war, however, Galena's economy took a sharp downturn, and by the end of the century, the forgotten town was nearly desolate.

In retrospect, being forgotten was probably the best thing that could have happened to Galena. Its splendid architectural masterpieces were left virtually untouched by the march of progress. U.S. Grant's family didn't even want to keep the Italian-style brick home the people of Galena presented to them in 1865. In 1904, nineteen years after Grant's death, his children donated it back.

COURTESY OF EAGLE RIDGE INN & RESORT

Today, 85 percent of the homes, churches, and government buildings in this nineteenth-century lead mining boom town are included in the National Register of Historic Places.

COURTESY OF EAGLE RIDGE INN & RESORT

Likewise, the county's familiar rolling hills, limestone bluffs, and great-grandfather oak trees were spared from the pressures of overdevelopment.

These pristine resources are now the pride of Eagle Ridge Inn & Resort, a golf mecca whose owners agreed it wasn't possible to improve on what Mother Nature had already done with the landscape. This exemplary approach has earned Eagle Ridge a long list of "best" awards since its opening in 1976.

Explorations of the resort's Old Stagecoach Trail (left) typically uncover curious woodchucks (top left), lively white-breasted nuthatches (top right), and delicate bloodroot (opposite page top) and sharp-lobed hepatica (opposite page bottom) flowers.

The 6,800-acre resort presents its players with sixty-three magnificent golf holes. The North Course, built to take advantage of the site's formidable hills and valleys, is especially beloved for its inspiring overlooks of Lake Galena. Roger Packard crafted this championship eighteen-hole layout, as well as its sister, the South Course. The South Course, the more heavily wooded of the two, embraces a scenic, yet diabolical little brook that wiggles through most of the acreage.

The East Course at Eagle Ridge is another complete test of golf. Its nine holes are fiercely defended by streams, ponds, forests, and rock outcroppings—hazards which demand a great deal of patience and precision.

Newest of the golf courses is The General. Designers Roger Packard and Andy North smartly fit their award-winning creation into the existing lay of the land. The location was naturally blessed with vigorous wetlands, hardy woodlands, spring-fed ponds, and jagged limestone cliffs. Very little of this terrain was altered. Even one of The General's man-made structures clearly demonstrates the resort's conservationist philosophy: an old farm silo was faithfully restored and then incorporated into the course's stylish clubhouse.

*Other trails tour the resort's signature
limestone sculptures (left) and furrowed watercourse (above).*

Both Eagle Ridge and Mother Nature have had a steadfast ally in Bob Graunke. Since the first shovel of earth was turned at the resort, he has been responsible for the vitality of its cherished ecosystems. During each course's construction, Graunke was able to shelter most of the native flora and fauna from the devastation of heavy equipment, and later replanted the habitats which were disturbed by the engineers and excavators. The understories of the deciduous forests Graunke helped to preserve are home to healthy populations of wild columbine, rock cress, purple cliffbrake fern, and American bladdernut.

Bob Graunke, Eagle Ridge's Director of Grounds, interprets The General's weathered rock faces.

The sunny hillsides bloom profusely with purple coneflower, wild bergamot, and germander; and the cooler north slopes support Dutchman's breeches, sharp-lobed hepatica, and wild ginger—to name only a few. The resort's forests grow an amazing assortment of indigenous trees, including eastern red cedar, quaking aspen, shagbark hickory, white oak, black cherry, slippery elm, green ash, sugar maple, black walnut, and American basswood.

Sunrise finds The General's opening hole gripped by a stubborn fog bank.

The clubhouse's distinctive grain silo guides play on The General's 9th hole.

The General #3

Tees on the par-three 14th offer up
sweeping views of The General's pastoral landscapes.

These woods and meadows ring with the calls of over forty-five bird species, among them: bald eagles, northern cardinals, cedar waxwings, eastern bluebirds, purple finches, snowy owls, wild turkeys, mourning doves, blue jays, and scarlet tanagers.

Graunke, as Director of Grounds for the resort, constantly monitors the integrity of water

sources, so that above- and below-ground springs will continue to flow clear and cold.

South Course #4

The 7th hole on the South Course (left) accommodates flocks of northern flickers (above) and American goldfinches (bottom).

134

Red baneberries (opposite page top left), wild geraniums (opposite page top right), and a tiny, twisting brook (opposite page bottom) enrich the edges of the South's 12th hole (above).

South Course #18

Furthermore, he convinced developers to maneuver around old growth forests, unique limestone formations, and a small patch of remnant prairie. Today, these unspoiled areas are conveniently accessed by the resort's impressive network of nature and leisure trails.

This abundance of carefully guarded wilderness forms a gentle backdrop for the resort's year-round array of family-oriented activities. Favorite pastimes include tennis, fishing, horseback riding, hiking, jogging, cycling, canoeing, sailing, sledding, skating, cross-country skiing, and sleigh-riding.

A white-tailed deer grazes in the meadowlands (above) adjacent to the East Course's 2nd hole (below).

East Course #3

While property owners and guests enjoy Eagle Ridge's idyllic surroundings, they also learn the importance of protecting places that soothe jangled nerves, places that nurture peaceful spirits...places the Winnebago might once again call "God's Country."

Once a noisy, bustling center of industry, the Vinegar Hill Lead Mine now serves as a window to the past.

Galena's nineteenth-century elegance is kept alive
by such historical structures as the Hellman (top left), Queen Anne (top right), and U.S. Grant (below) houses.

Sunset from Eagle Ridge's Stony Point Lookout

GRAND VIEW LODGE

Sunrise sparkles across the resort's Gull Lake.

*I*ronically, when it was named Grand View Lodge in 1916, the logging companies had so thoroughly cleared the landscape that "you could stand on a gopher hill, let alone some noble glacial kame, and see forever."

Today, Grand View Lodge, near Brainerd, Minnesota, is described by *Home & Garden* magazine as "a floral masterpiece of the northland," and by *Golf Digest* and *Golf Magazine* as one of America's finest golf resorts.

The region's reputation as a center of hospitality began well over a century ago, when the lakes of northern Minnesota teemed with fish and game—and the sportsmen who came to take the wildlife. Their first hunting camps were mostly small, primitive *wannigans* (shelters), but a whole resort industry soon grew up around the concept of providing the travelers with more substantial and convenient housing and meals.

One such early resort area was Gull Lake, near the town of Nisswa. In his spirited collection of stories called *Oldtimers*, local historian Carl A. Zapffe relates that the south end of Gull Lake boasted a number of popular resorts by the turn of the century. Pine Beach Hotel (featuring a golf course and platted lots) Ozonite Park, and Rocky Point Resort were all attracting plenty of tourists.

The time was World War I, and financial fortunes were as fickle as the fortunes of war. Land known as the Bergh estate went into foreclosure, and following a fast paced series of sales, defaults, and resales, came under simultaneous ownership between Marvin Baker and Henry Spalding.

144

Henry Spalding was a retired county sheriff as well as the long-time proprietor of the Spalding Hotel in Crosby. Believing he had clear title, he converted the old Bergh estate into a commodious hunting cabin in 1915, and then obtained a quitclaim deed.

Imposing stands of timber dwarf the Woods' par-three 3rd hole.

The Woods #9

Enter Marvin Baker, a former telegraph operator from Columbus, Ohio. Eager to make his fortune without the grind of twelve-hour days at the key, Baker moved from Columbus to Minneapolis and went into real estate sales with Harry Seaton. On a fishing trip with conservationist Frank Lees, Baker toured Gull Lake and learned that the Bergh place was on the market.

Nearby, the Bishop homestead had recently been surveyed for subdivision, and a plat had been completed on a neighboring acreage. Buyers seemed to be standing in line, and the scent of profit was in the wind.

Baker and Seaton acquired the foreclosed Bergh property through an agent named Braithwaite; at the same time, Spalding purchased the estate through an agent named Brundage. While legal arguments progressed, Baker and Seaton continued to secure additional holdings in the county, but refused to give up their claim to the Bergh title.

Finally, in April of 1916, Spalding's failing health convinced him to give up the fight. He kept a few acres for himself and sold the others to Baker for $6,200. The plat for Gull Lake Park was filed within the month, and Baker's dream began to come true—although not without many twelve-hour-plus days.

Baker required a place for his prospective lot buyers to stay, so he enlarged and upgraded Spalding's hunting cabin, renaming it Grand View Lodge. Shortly before the official opening, he married Harriett Menk and immediately appointed her the retreat's first cook and hostess. Baker bought a motor launch to transport visitors across Gull Lake to his lodge, and then persuaded the electric company to bring in service from the highway. His real estate business flourished.

Marvin Baker, described by some acquaintances and friends as "a sharpie who lived off his wits," moved quickly when the war ended and the economy boomed.

Birdhouses (right),
blue jays (above),
and cedar waxwings (top)
flank the course's fairways.

The Lakes' par-three 7th hole is guarded from tee to green by a menacing little pond.

Adjacent to the course, Roy Lake (bottom) accommodates the resort's American widgeons (above right) and pintail ducks (above left).

Realizing that more and more people would be looking for quiet destinations to spend their holidays, he made plans for the construction of a truly magnificent lodge. The present Grand View Lodge rose log by log, and on June 1, 1921, the three-storey structure was ready to welcome vacationers.

Hilltop teeboxes on the Marsh's par-three 5th hole overlook the course's pristine wetlands.

Baker took a keen interest in marketing his lodge, which featured a nickelodeon and large dance floor for guests' entertainment. He would often stroll into the ballroom with a hatful of nickels to get the action started, a tactic which proved to be highly successful.

Northern pitcher plants (left) and blue flag irises (right) further enhance the spectacular setting.

Sadly, his most ambitious promotion would turn into his most dismal failure. In an effort to extend the tourist season beyond the pleasant summer months, he organized a Labor Day weekend speedboat race. Northern Minnesota can be decidedly chilly by Labor Day, and this particular year was no exception. Determined to draw a huge crowd, Baker spent a great deal of money on the event's advertising and prizes.

The Marsh #3

A series of bunkers tighten up the approach to the Marsh's 7th green.

COURTESY OF GRAND VIEW LODGE

On the morning of the race, the weather over Gull Lake was steely, wet, cold, and windy. Only three boats showed up to compete, and only Baker stood on shore to watch. He gamely heaped the prizes on all three shivering participants, but it was a terribly bitter and expensive lesson.

A little more than a decade after they erected it, the Bakers sold Grand View Lodge to R.F.B. Cote. Today, the venerable old lodge (listed on the National Register of Historic Places) continues to be owned and administered by the Cote family.

West of the resort, the last traces of northern Minnesota's first residents are maintained and interpreted by the U.S. Army Corps of Engineers. The Gull Lake

Burial Mounds Trail leads to the sacred graves of the Woodland Indians who lived here in permanent settlements from 1000 B.C. to A.D. 1700. Twelve large mounds and a number of smaller ones rest along the location's shaded footpaths. From the unearthed pottery fragments, stone tools, and human and animal bones, archeologists have been able to piece together a better understanding of these ancient inhabitants.

The colorful beginnings of Crow Wing County's logging industry are also remembered, punctuated by folklore of such bigger than life heroes as Paul Bunyan. Two important community projects were even named to honor the legendary woodsman. The Paul Bunyan Trail, developed by the Minnesota Department of Natural Resources and Waterways, was once an active line for the Burlington Northern Railroad, but now the scenic 100-mile-long route serves the county's cyclists and snowmobilers. The 583-acre Paul Bunyan Arboretum is highlighted by 3,000 different species of plants and sixteen miles of hiking and cross-country skiing trails. To protect the habitats of local wildlife populations, the majority of the arboretum has been kept in its native state.

The lush understories of The Preserve's 10th (opposite page bottom) and 17th (opposite page top) holes grow a broad range of regional flora, including harebells (above right), wood lilies (left), and wild sunflowers (above left).

GRAND VIEW LODGE: CHAPTER 7

*Set in the shadow of the rustic Grand View Lodge (above), the Kids Club
entertains youngsters with an array of outdoor programs and projects (top and bottom right).*

Carved into a sweet-smelling evergreen forest, Grand
View's nine-hole Garden Course has been in operation
since 1918. But to keep up with the surging popularity
of the game of golf, the resort had eighteen holes of
The Pines in play by 1991, and introduced a third nine in 1994. The Lakes, Woods, and
Marsh nines were created to take full advantage of the existing topography.

Designer Joel Goldstrand dramatically blended the site's water, rocks, and woods into his twenty-seven holes of championship golf. The 340-acre tract takes golfers over gently rolling fairways; past towering stands of pine, birch, and aspen; along the margins of unspoiled marshes; and through meadows of indigenous grasses and wild-

flowers. In recognition of its stellar environmental practices, The Pines was designated a Cooperative Sanctuary by the Audubon Society in 1995.

In the fall of 1996, the resort presented its players with another exhilarating test of golf. The eighteen-hole, 240-acre Preserve course features eleven elevated teeboxes, thirty-six perfectly positioned sand traps, and forty acres of prime wetlands.

The Gull Lake Burial Mounds Trail (below) supports caches of mayapples (above right) and fairy slippers (above left).

Just south of Grand View's lakes and forests, a red-tailed hawk (below) surveys the perimeter of a vast sunflower field (above).

Grand View Lodge also takes care of tennis enthusiasts. Its professional teaching staff and eleven Laykold courts have placed the property on *Tennis* magazine's list of the fifty best tennis resorts in the United States.

The resort's Gull Lake is an especially busy spot during the high season. A shimmering 1,500-foot-long sandy beach attracts swimmers and suntanners; motor launches, sail boats, canoes, and kayaks indulge sightseers, and walleye of lunker proportions tempt anglers.

The trees have grown back at Grand View Lodge, and floral displays are still a part of its rich legacy of hospitality. It is a delightful result of cultural and ecological preservation that valued traditions prevail and community stability emerges. Many homes built in the earliest days of the resort still stand, and many of the first lots purchased are now owned by second- and third-generation members of the original families.

West of Gull Lake, Pillsbury State Forest contains 1,500 acres of glacier-shaped hills (below), lakes, ponds, and streams.

Pillsbury's Green Bass Lake presents hikers with beaver lodges (above),
redhead ducks (top right), and masses of fragrant water lilies (bottom right).

Daylight quietly wanes over Gull Lake.

THE AMERICAN CLUB/ BLACKWOLF RUN

Opened in 1918 to board Kohler Co.'s immigrant employees, The American Club today operates as one of the country's finest resort hotels.

A tiny Midwestern village near the Sheboygan River in Wisconsin is a living example of patriotism. John Michael Kohler emigrated as a young man from the Bregenzerwald, Austria, to the United States in the mid-1800s. With an unshakeable commitment to excellence and hard work, he began manufacturing farming equipment in the heart of dairy country, a venture that would prove to be extremely successful.

The success story, however, did not occur overnight. The business he established in 1873 was dogged first by a depression, and then by a fire that destroyed the newly expanded machine shop. The disaster only made Kohler more determined. He decided to diversify, adding enameled plumbing fixtures to the existing agricultural lines. Kohler Co. was soon turning out thousands of sinks, bathtubs, kettles, and pans; and before long, the new products were outselling the original lines.

John's eldest son, Walter, kept the company in the avant-garde after his father's death. To help other immigrants succeed, he built an impressive Tudor-style manor to serve as an affordable boarding house. Food expenses were minimal since the Kohler farm supplied vegetables, butter, eggs, and milk to the vast storage rooms of the kitchen. The American Club was famous for the tables it laid, groaning with abundance even during the Great Depression.

In 1917, Walter asked the Olmsted Bros. firm of Brookline, Massachusetts to organize the town that was growing up around the Kohler factory. Riverside became one of the first planned communities in the United States, and would later adopt the name of its founding family.

The Village of Kohler was everything a company town should be. Wholesome entertainment was provided for the employees: billiards, bowling, baseball leagues, concerts, and special holiday celebrations.

Blackwolf Run's hardwood stands and rippled plateaus shape the Meadow Valleys' 10th hole.

After both World Wars, the Kohler Building and Loan Association helped returning soldiers purchase reasonably priced housing in the village. And, at the center of it all, was Walter's symbol of national pride: a 100-foot flagpole for the Stars and Stripes, which still waves its salute to the land of opportunity.

Kohler's industries continue to drive the village's economy, but today its fiscal stability is supplemented by The American Club. The Gold Medal property has been dubbed by *Golf Magazine* as "a superlative resort that never rests in its quest for excellence." Listed on the National Register of Historic Places, the former boarding house is now the Midwest's only AAA Five Diamond resort hotel. Walter Kohler's dream of creating a place "dedicated to the enhancement of gracious living" is alive and well at The American Club and in the Village of Kohler.

COURTESY OF KOHLER CO.

The village also contains a sentimental memorial to the late founder of Kohler Co., John Michael Kohler. The Waelderhaus, a three-storey homestead emulating the nineteenth-century trends and traditions of western Austria, was born out of Marie Kohler's wish to honor the achievements of her father. To bring her vision to fruition, Marie engaged the expertise of Austrian-born artisan and architect Kaspar Albrecht. Kaspar faithfully designed the structure, supervised its construction, and even rendered its reliefs, carvings, woodcuts, and sculptures.

Meadow Valleys' par-three 3rd hole

The Waelderhaus was officially opened to the public on July 26, 1931. Guided tours of the beloved home are highlighted by viewings of the Baden-Powell Room, named for the British general who originated the Scouting movement in 1908. Styled after a medieval guild hall, the room is filled with Girl Scout tributes, from the coats of arms on the walls to the merit badges cut into the iron chandeliers to the stained-glass windows depicting the three figures of Faith, Hope, and Charity.

The course's sprawling grasslands (below) harbor a white-tailed doe (above left) and her shy fawn (above right).

Other village attractions include the Kohler Design Center, a 36,000-square-foot exhibition of the company's past, present, and future; Artspace, a gallery of the John Michael Kohler Arts Center; the Inn on Woodlake, another exquisite hotel; Sports Core, the resort's health club and spa; and The Shops at Woodlake Kohler, a selection of tasteful boutiques and restaurants.

River Wildlife, a private 500-acre wilderness preserve, invites members to shoot, hike, ride horseback, and cross-country ski on thirty miles of marked trails; its seven miles of rivers and streams are popular with canoeists and fishermen. Perfectly complementing its wooded surroundings, the preserve's rustic log cabin charms its guests with a massive fieldstone fireplace, a splendid dining room, and a stunning collection of naturalist artworks.

Two nearby state parks showcase the region's unique landforms: Kohler Andrae State Park, a 750-acre parcel noted for its shifting sand dunes; and Kettle Moraine State Forest, a 43,000-acre timberland revered for its tranquil lakes, nature trails, and picnic spots. Three village parks—Ravine, Roosevelt, and Lost Woods—and the Old Plank Road Trail offer pathways for walking, jogging, and cycling.

Butterfly weed (above) and purple coneflowers (right) pattern the course's naturalized margins.

Weeden's Creek snakes maniacally around the Meadow Valleys' 14th green (above).

The creek is resourcefully spanned by an old railroad flatcar.

Even the village's outskirts are park-like. The entry road to the golf courses is bordered by a specially designed prairie planting, an ongoing project of the Kohler Co. Landscape Department's architects, horticulturists, and arborists. Indigenous flowers and grasses dress up the roadway and golf courses, producing a striking contrast between the manicured and the unmanaged.

An early morning fog bank softly envelops the Meadow Valleys' daunting par-three 15th.   COURTESY OF KOHLER CO.

A fountain garden (above) and a symbolic flagpole (right) grace The American Club's grounds.

The Waelderhaus introduces visitors to the distinctive customs of western Austria, the ancestral home of the Kohler family.

Plant materials were chosen based on their abilities to resist pests, wind, cold, heat, and drought. The windswept meadows flourish from spring to fall with tens of thousands of hardy wildflowers.

Within The American Club, plantings are more structured. To provide its guests with quiet meditative space, the hotel's main wings are separated by four formal courtyard gardens.

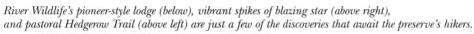

River Wildlife's pioneer-style lodge (below), vibrant spikes of blazing star (above right), and pastoral Hedgerow Trail (above left) are just a few of the discoveries that await the preserve's hikers.

Just down the way, the Kohler Gardener outlet maintains a fascinating butterfly garden for people's enjoyment and education. Encircled by stone walkways and wrought-iron benches, the beds attract the flighty insects with a spectacular array of sweet-scented flora. To replenish population levels, the chrysalides of native butterflies are frequently transplanted into the garden; hibernation boxes help them survive the chilly winters.

While the resort was "dedicated to the enhancement of gracious living," the golf courses were dedicated to the advancement of a player's skills. When designer Pete Dye first surveyed the pristine 400-acre site (named for Black Wolf, a fearsome Winnebago warrior chief), he was moved to remark: "There could not be a better natural setting for golf."

Beautiful arrangements of common wood sorrel (below left) and wild blue phlox (below right) color Blackwolf Trail's overgrown footpath (above).

THE AMERICAN CLUB/BLACKWOLF RUN: CHAPTER 8

Enormous pit bunkers and tightly clustered hillocks guard the River Course's 2nd green.

Dye carefully laid out Blackwolf Run's thirty-six unforgettable golf holes so that they all would flow easily with the existing terrain.

174

*The woods flanking the right side of the River Course's 17th hole (top)
support masses of ferns (above) and Canada violets (right).*

The River Course is biennially ranked high on *Golf Digest*'s list of "America's 100 Greatest Golf Courses." Its tumbling fairways serve up unobstructed views of the Sheboygan River's breathtaking twists and turns. The river dominates the landscape—coming into play on ten holes—but the challenge is sharply reinforced by fifty-foot bluffs, giant cottonwoods, swollen knolls, punishing bunkers, and roller-coaster greens.

River Course #10   COURTESY OF KOHLER CO.

A young red-tailed hawk feeds on the frogs beside the hole's forward tee.

The 9th's tall back tees tempt players to hit across a scenic bend in the Sheboygan River.   COURTESY OF KOHLER CO.

The Meadow Valleys Course was dramatically carved out of strapping hills, grass-covered plains, and rugged post-glacial ridges, gullies, and ravines.

River Course #13

While longer than the River Course, straight-shooters usually find the Meadow Valleys Course to be slightly less vexing. The more wayward players, however, are often spotted wandering through the course's chest-high rough alongside the resort's white-tailed deer.

Decorated with an intriguing assortment of nineteenth-century Native American artifacts, Blackwolf Run's magnificent lodgepole log clubhouse coordinates the golf operations from its hilltop perch.

The attention lavished on the resort's guests is a testament to the attention Walter Kohler lavished on the company's employees. Each time one of the factory's immigrant workers became a United States citizen, his photograph would be proudly displayed at the boarding house. Even when plans were launched to convert the boarding house into a luxurious hotel, the cherished portraits were removed, stored, and later replaced once renovations were finished.

Resort restaurants, too, exhibit cultural pride. The Horse & Plow's casual decor is reminiscent of a turn-of-the-century British pub. The Greenhouse, a charming antique solarium imported from England, is now a delectable Victorian dessert parlor. The Winery's lounge, modeled after European wine cellars, is located adjacent to The Immigrant Restaurant, formerly the boarding house's laundry.

Wild crocuses (top), Indian pipes (right),
and New England asters (above) adorn the hole's dense forests.

The Sheboygan River's gentle currents (above) offer sanctuary to a bathing eastern meadowlark (below left) and a drifting black duck (below right).

Today, its six dining rooms reflect six different ethnic backgrounds of Kohler's first European settlers: French, Dutch, German Hunt, Normandy, Scandinavian, and English heritages are warmly represented. The elegant Wisconsin Room boasts leaded-glass windows, oak wood paneling, thematic tapestries, crystal chandeliers, and drawings of distinguished Wisconsin citizens. A glass panel above the room's entryway is inscribed with a John Ruskin quote that expresses one of Walter Kohler's strongest beliefs: "Life without labor is guilt, labor without art is brutality."

Visitors to The American Club would surely agree that Walter lived up to his ambition of presenting a good impression of America to all who cross his threshold.

Dusk streaks the horizon over the River Course.

BOYNE USA RESORTS

Boyne's setting is naturally blessed by Lake Michigan's unspoiled dunes and towering evergreens.

By the mid-1980s, the limestone was played out and the quarrying equipment was obsolete. The chalky bones of the Earth were plainly visible where her trees and topsoil had been blasted away; skeletons of once-productive buildings stood empty and forgotten. Yet all around the mined-out remains—like the cake surrounding the hole in a doughnut—the clear blue waters of Lake Michigan sparkled at the feet of robust green hills.

It took ten years, an act of legislation, and millions of dollars to convert this depleted northern Michigan industrial site into one of the country's most desirable resorts: Bay Harbor. Today, nouveau Victorian mansions grace the 1,100 acres of bluffs and valleys where stone crushers had thundered. The deep quarry pond is now a marina and yacht club. Bay Harbor's five miles of Great Lake shoreline have been miraculously restored and reforested. Its collection of three world-class nine-hole golf courses showcase the diverse terrain as it shifts from fragile beach dunes to rugged quarry cliffs to heavy stands of birch and cedar.

Northeast of Bay Harbor, across the broad expanse of Little Traverse Bay, the colorful town of Harbor Springs continues to nurture the area's reputation as a resort destination; a reputation that began in the 1860s, when such private associations as The Chicago Club, Belvedere, Bay View, Wequetonsing, Menonaqua, and Harbor Point were founded.

Centuries earlier, the first humans to see this wild landscape were living within its thriving forests and next to its crystal lakes and streams. Anthropologists refer to these original residents as Woodland Indians, but they called themselves *Anishnabek*—meaning simply "the people." The Anishnabek, or more specifically the Odawa (Ottawa), Ojibwa (Chippewa), and Potawatomi tribes, formed a confederation known as the "Three Fires". The fertile soil and temperate offshore breezes were ideally suited to their way of life.

The Ojibwa were primarily hunters, the Odawa traders, and the Potawatomi agriculturists. Because of their close proximity to major waterway systems, they would eventually be "discovered" by Europeans pushing west in an effort to claim the vast riches of the uncharted continent. Contact with whites occurred around 1615, when French fur traders paddled their canoes down through the bountiful Canadian wilderness to Sault Ste. Marie, south to the Straits of Mackinac, then along Michigan's northwest shore.

Reedy ponds and vigorous woods guard The Heather's 4th (below) and 5th (opposite page) holes.

The explorers brought with them an enticing selection of tools, blankets, and trinkets—goods the Anishnabek would come to treasure. These foreign wares became an important leg in a triangle of commerce: the Odawa offered their handmade baskets, utensils, and garments to the Ojibwa for furs, and then dealt the furs to the French to procure their precious commodities.

The Heather #9

As the French and Native American cultures intermingled, their languages found common ground. What the Odawa called *waw gaw naw kezee*, the French called *L'Arbre Croche*—both phrases referring to a landmark "crooked tree" that bent out over Lake Michigan near what is now Harbor Springs. The French *bon jour* was the Indian *boo shoo*, the greeting many Anishnabek still use when speaking to non-natives.

Soon, canoes transported not only traders in search of goods to amass, but also Jesuit priests in search of souls to save. The "black robes" established missions in Cross Village, Harbor Springs, and Middle Village (so named because it was positioned halfway between the two larger settlements). The three Catholic mission churches—Middle Village's St. Ingatius, Harbor Spring's Holy Childhood, and Cross Village's St. Clement—continue to minister to the remaining members of the Odawa Nation here in their ancient homeland.

Sadly, that same homeland was all but lost under the presidency of Andrew Jackson. The federal government's policy was to relocate all indigenous peoples living east of the Mississippi to "worthless" territories in Kansas and Oklahoma. Those who walked the "Trail of Tears" declared that the flat, arid plains were incapable of sustaining life. Only a few scattered bands of Odawa were able to avoid expulsion. Assisted by the powerful Catholic Church, careful political maneuvering secured them small reservations in the state. The Church then became involved in programs to assimilate the natives into the burgeoning white communities.

White-tailed deer (top) and wild turkeys (bottom) share The Heather course with the resort's golfers.

RANDY McCUNE, NATURAL EXPRESSIONS LTD.

186

RANDY McCUNE, NATURAL EXPRESSIONS LTD.

BOYNE USA RESORTS: CHAPTER 9

The Heather #17

Church officials provided seeds, livestock, lumber, and education, but attempted to take away languages, beliefs, laws, and practices.

One practice in particular was routinely disregarded by greedy white entrepreneurs. The social structure of the Odawa required decisions to be reached by consensus. The tribal chief, though greatly respected, possessed no authority to enter his people into obligatory contracts. If a brave disagreed with his chief, he simply would not comply. In more serious disputes, dissidents would break away and join others who held similar views. On rare occasions, leaders were even put to death for repeatedly ignoring the wishes of the majority. So, while serving as role models in societal and personal matters, chiefs wielded very little real power to act on behalf of the group. Land grant treaties signed by an individual of the tribe—which the whites considered legal and binding—were invalid according to the ways of the Odawa.

A menacing storm front grips the skies above The Moor's 16th hole.

White baneberries (top) and high-domed mushrooms (above) push through the leaf litter of The Moor's 7th hole (left).

Before long, another generation of Odawa found themselves expelled from the places they had cherished for centuries. In peaceful meadows where blackberries once grew, fence posts now sprouted from the ground. Maple trees which had yielded sugary sap were felled and shipped to faraway cities. The deer and partridge lost much of their wooded habitats. Even the passenger pigeons—at one time more plentiful than mosquitoes—gradually vanished.

Both the challenge and the aesthetic of The Moor's closing hole are dominated by a placid reflecting pond.

Nevertheless, a number of Anishnabek families were able to retain modest acreages in the area. Harbor Springs, formerly the capital of the Odawa Nation, is still called home by today's tribe; and it is still an active center of trade, attracting discerning collectors with exquisite native crafts fashioned from birch bark, porcupine quills, rawhide, cattails, clay, cedar, and black ash. The lakeside town is also a glittering stage where time-honored traditions—once forbidden—are again celebrated. Each year, the Odawa organize a homecoming powwow in Harbor Springs to welcome back far-flung members of their nation and to renew the experience of their rich heritage.

*Fall foliage
(left and bottom left)
and American kestrels
(bottom right) dress up
Harbor Springs' back roads.*

Over the past 125 years, a people called "resorters" have come to appreciate the region's wild abundance. In arranging the land to fit their desires, the more considerate developers have strived to maintain this splendid natural history.

So it is that in the fall, when the morning air is decidedly crisp and the evenings are filled with curls of fragrant woodsmoke, northern Michigan's storied hardwoods continue to enrichen the countryside with their invigorating colors; and following the stubborn winters, springtime still replenishes forest floors with showy carpets of trillium flowers and tasty crops of morel mushrooms.

Highlights of trendy Harbor Springs include its Holy Childhood Church (top left), municipal marina (top right), and quaint turn-of-the-century cottages (right).

In the midst of these earthly delicacies exist some of the most sought-after inventions of mankind: ski hills and golf courses. The first of these came to be when a young Everett Kircher left his job selling Studebakers in Detroit to start up a small ski operation near Boyne City. His Boyne Mountain resort opened in 1947, and backed by the success of that venture, a second ski facility, Boyne Highlands, was launched sixteen years later. Together, "The Boynes" pioneered the area's hospitality industry.

Both Boynes were engineered to take advantage of the glacier-formed hills at the tip of Michigan's mitten. But to hold on to his valued winter help, Kircher needed to provide them with year-round employment. He decided to extend the utility of his ski resorts by introducing recreational pursuits for the other three seasons as well.

Bird feeders in the vicinity of The Donald Ross Memorial's 1st (below)
and 3rd (opposite page top) holes accommodate the local blue jays (above) and white-breasted nuthatches (opposite page bottom).

What served as ski hills in the winter became the foundation for golf courses in the spring, summer, and fall. Golf may have begun as a way to keep ski staff employed twelve months a year, but it quickly became the cornerstone of Boyne's summer economy.

With the dedication of The Heather course in 1965, Boyne Highlands was acknowledged as Michigan's first public golf resort. Its formidable Robert Trent Jones, Sr. layout tours players past hardwood groves, cranberry bogs, cedar swamps, cattail-rimmed ponds, and wildflower-strewn meadows. These natural assets, combined with its sculpted bunkers and greens, have kept The Heather ranked with the state's top courses.

194

The Moor was the next course to open at Boyne Highlands. Conceived by William Newcomb in 1974, nearly every hole is challenged by water in one form or another, from native wetlands to man-made lakes and ponds. Home of the Michigan PGA Championship, The Moor is further distinguished by acute doglegs, penal sand traps, and roller-coaster putting surfaces.

When The Donald Ross Memorial course was completed at the Highlands in 1989, it immediately earned rave reviews for its brilliant tribute to the game's legendary architect. Everett Kircher, his son Stephen, William Newcomb, and golf instructor Jim Flick conducted extensive research before breaking ground at the site, which now features eighteen authentic re-creations of some of Donald Ross's greatest golf holes chosen from such venerable courses as Inverness, Plainfield, Aronimink, Seminole, Oakland Hills, Pinehurst No. 2, and Royal Dornoch.

The Donald Ross Memorial #6

The Donald Ross Memorial #8

The Arthur Hills #2

Newest in the Highlands' repertoire is The Arthur Hills course—named for its accomplished designer. Routed alongside teeming bogs, oak thickets, and pine-covered hills, the burly 7,037-yard tract opened nine of its eighteen holes in 1997.

Boyne Highlands' southern sister, Boyne Mountain, boasts two superb eighteen-hole layouts. An exhilarating mile-long cart ride to the summit of Boyne Mountain moves players to the opening holes. The 7,086-yard Monument course is especially beloved for its dramatically elevated teeboxes, heavily contoured fairways, and feeling of complete isolation.

The Alpine course at Boyne Mountain was built to capture the picture-perfect views of the neighboring hills and lakes, views which can distract even the most unflappable golfer. At every turn of its 7,017 yards, inviting fairways can lull challengers into a false bubble of security that is often burst by strategically positioned sand traps and water hazards.

North of the resort, autumn's glorious hues cloak the quiet country lanes.

Further north, Sturgeon Bay's magnificent lake shore (above) and sand dunes (below) lie within the protective confines of Wilderness State Park, a pristine 8,000-acre refuge.

Eons of wind and waves have randomly shaped the dunes (above) and polished the rocks (below) along Wilderness's Waugoshance Point.

While the evolution of the two Boynes has been remarkable, the resort's most amazing accomplishment to date is still its Bay Harbor development. Pretentiously dubbed the "queen of debutantes" by an ambitious writer, Bay Harbor is, nonetheless, an extraordinary piece of real estate snatched from the grasp of industrial decay and financial neglect.

When the last nine of Bay Harbor's twenty-seven holes opened in 1998, Arthur Hills' breath-

taking creation was instantly hailed as a modern-day masterpiece. The three dynamic nine-hole courses—The Links, The Quarry, and The Preserve—play between 10 to 150 feet above the property's broad beaches.

The Links at Bay Harbor #4

BOYNE USA RESORTS: CHAPTER 9

The shimmering waters of Little Traverse Bay backdrop the 1st (above) and 3rd (below) holes of The Links course.

Hardy clumps of black-eyed Susans (below) flourish beside The Links' 7th green (above).

Offering panoramic views of Little Traverse Bay, six of The Links' holes sweep along 2.5 miles of scenic shoreline—the longest of any course in the country. The Preserve's nine holes trek through hundreds of acres of second growth timberland, while five holes of the aptly named Quarry are directly influenced by the former cement plant's craggy limestone cliffs.

202

A glassy trout pond reflects the lights of the ivy-covered Highlands Inn.

People are beginning to understand how fortunate the Indians were to have had a living relationship with Mother Earth. Over the last couple of decades, golfers are discovering that their sport can help to re-establish these bonds, and that the natural lay of the land can reinforce the enjoyment of the game.

Just north of Harbor Springs, the Thorne Swift Nature Preserve presents sightseers with spectacular Lake Michigan sunsets.

CHATEAU WHISTLER
RESORT

The looming peaks of the Coast Mountains watch over picturesque Whistler Village.

*F*ew places exist where one can play eighteen holes of championship golf on a mid-June morning, and then ski a 12,000-year-old glacier in the afternoon. Head for Whistler, British Columbia, however, and you'd be wise to pack your clubs and skis. Chateau Whistler Resort serves up both diversions.

Chateau Whistler Resort is set into the spectacular valley between Whistler and Blackcomb Mountains, seventy-five miles north of Vancouver, British Columbia. This craggy mountain location is home to the number-one-ranked ski resort in North America, famous for its mile-high vertical rise and eight-month-long season.

At the base of the mountains, below stark granite ledges and great stands of Douglas fir, lies Chateau Whistler's world renowned golf course. The glorious Robert Trent Jones, Jr. design makes full use of the valley's premier assets: dense evergreen forests, rolling foothills, rushing streams, reflective ponds, and weathered rock outcroppings. When it debuted in 1993, the facility's dramatic combination of scenery and challenge helped it earn *Golf Digest*'s "Best New Canadian Course" award.

In 1998, Chateau Whistler Golf Club became only the ninth course in Canada to be certified by the Audubon Cooperative Sanctuary System—a fitting tribute to those who had lavished so much care and attention on the layout and its ecology. Under the directive of superintendent Bert McFadden and lead hand Rick Monroe, the club's maintenance policies have been vigilantly expanded over the years to deal with issues such as water quality testing, wildlife habitat protection and enhancement, environmental planning practices, and public awareness programs.

Several concerned local organizations supplement the golf club's efforts. Most noticeably, the Whistler Fisheries Stewardship group, the Whistler Angling Club, the Resort Municipality of Whistler, and the Whistler Rotary Club work together to ensure the purity of water sources and to monitor the vitality of fish populations.

Chateau Whistler Golf Club's 2nd green is tightly guarded by the tumbling waters and rocky banks of Horstman Creek.

On the edges of this exclusive resort are countless other breathtaking natural phenomena, including: Singing Pass, a mountain gap adored for its springtime carpet of wildflowers; Cheakamus Lake, a glacier-fed reservoir teeming with rainbow trout and Dolly Varden; Cougar Mountain, a preserve for 1,000-year-old giant cedar trees; The Barrier, an impervious lava dam holding back Garibaldi Lake; and Black Tusk, a majestic lava pinnacle enveloped by unspoiled highlands.

All of these elements converge in the towering Coast Mountains, part of the geological chain that also includes Mt. St. Helens, Mt. Rainier, Mt. Baker, and the San Andreas fault. Stretching from North Vancouver to Alaska, the Coast Mountains were sculpted by fire and ice as the volcanoes and glaciers left their marks in the granite. During the last ten millennia, the forest claimed a foothold in the terrain from which the glaciers receded, conceiving a delightfully wild and diverse landscape. Its stunning beauty, at once rugged and fragile, has made it a treasured retreat for nearly a century.

Early on, part of Whistler's appeal was its comparative remoteness. The first path through the mountain passes was known as the Squamish/Pemberton Trail, blazed by the natives as a trade route. Later, gold seekers, trappers, and miners marked and widened the path until it was decreed an official road by the government of British Columbia in 1891. It was surely a road like no other, however: only two feet wide in most sections, and prone to flooding, washouts, dead falls, and rock slides.

Meadows featuring tall spikes of lupine (left) and fireweed (above) border the course's fairways.

LEANNA RATHKELLY

*Ox-eye daisies flourish
throughout the hole's naturalized zones.*

LEANNA RATHKELLY

During the first decade of this century, it was an arduous two-day climb up the mountain to John Miller's rest house at Whistler's Alta Lake. Alex and Myrtle Philip, friends of the Millers, would also establish a history of hospitality in the area. The Philips made annual visits to Whistler, found the journey to be most invigorating, and in 1914, acquired a nearby fishing camp. Later that same year, they opened Rainbow Lodge and shared their beloved mountain life with other adventurers.

209

When the Pacific Great Eastern Railway arrived in 1914, Whistler's backcountry became accessible to greater numbers of people. Other fishing lodges were constructed, and with word spreading rapidly of the natural splendor, Alta Lake soon became the most popular vacation spot west of Alberta's Banff and Jasper National Parks.

Chateau Whistler's 15th (opposite page) and 7th (above) holes present players with rigorous elevation changes and inspiring panoramic views.

Interest in the region further intensified once the old road from the ocean to the interior valleys—the Sea to Sky Highway—was upgraded for automobile traffic. With transportation now an easier proposition, more and more travelers made the trek to the mountains not only for the fishing, but now for the skiing as well.

The 8th hole's rocky knoll (below) is brought to life by showy California poppies (right) and a basking hoary marmot (far right).

Bunkers on the 14th hole emulate the snow-capped peaks of the neighboring mountain ranges.

During the 1960s and 1970s, Stefan Ples and Franz Wilhelmsen developed the ski industry

in Whistler, introducing the lifts which were needed to accommodate the swelling crowds.

The par-three 16th

Beauty and recreation were not, however, all that these mountains had to offer. The railroad may have brought tourists in, but it also took logs and lumber out.

*Yellow skunk cabbage (left) and cinnamon teal (above)
thrive in the wetlands alongside the course's Horstman Creek (below).*

When truck access improved, the mountainsides were even more aggressively scoured for their abundant reserves of timber and minerals.

During this period of hasty expansion, many hard lessons were learned. By the 1980s, it was evident that logging companies needed to be regulated if the forest was to renew itself, and that the ecology needed to be conserved if tourism was to remain healthy.

To appease both sightseers and loggers, the Resort Municipality of Whistler, the British Columbia Ministry of Forests, and the Pacific Forest Products Ltd. teamed up to innovate a 7,400-acre interpretive forest dedicated to resource management studies.

The 18th's enormous green is dramatically backdropped by the resort's distinctive clubhouse and hotel.

After a game of golf, the Green River (below) and Lost Lake (above) help to reinforce the outdoors experience.

Situated in the upper Cheakamus Valley, the Whistler Interpretive Forest is a "living classroom" of logging demonstration sites and educational trails and stations. The location encompasses two biogeoclimatic zones: the Coastal Western Hemlock Zone (the most productive timber belt in Canada) and the Mountain Hemlock Zone. The wild and diverse character of the mountains is once again being reclaimed—in this case not from glaciers and volcanoes, but from the occurrences of destructive land use practices.

216

The 7th Heaven Express chair lift transports riders up to Blackcomb Mountain's Horstman Hut, where icy summits (above and below) may be explored with experienced guides.

Today, logging companies must replant their harvested blocks and then take care of the young trees until they reach their "free growing" stage. Slash is removed from the forest floor to lessen the risk of fires. Cut block dimensions are kept smaller and are now more discreetly chosen. Also, a variety of updated thinning and pruning techniques are being employed to minimize the adverse consequences of forestry operations.

ISOBEL MACLAURIN

Singing Pass Trail (below) is highlighted by delicate white heather blossoms (top right), lively western bluebirds (right), and colorful tiger lilies (below right).

218

ISOBEL MACLAURIN

For its part, Chateau Whistler Resort has organized a special environmental committee of service staff and supervisory personnel to oversee the demanding, double-edged mission of promoting and protecting the area's pristine wilderness.

Visitors can take a gondola to the top of a mountain or play a round of golf in the valley; hike to tremendous waterfalls or bike through alpine heaths; climb a rock face or kayak a river; ride a horse or return a serve; soar under a paraglider or maneuver on a snowboard; hook a sockeye salmon or sight a massive black bear; bundle up for a walk across a glacier or dress down for a stroll along a beach.

The Whistler Interpretive Forest embraces vast timberlands (top), serrated granite walls (above), cinnamon-colored black bears (right), placid Logger's Lake (opposite page top), and the powerful Cheakamus River (opposite page bottom).

For even quieter times, Chateau Whistler Resort offers its guests elegant restaurants and boutiques, an indoor-outdoor pool and whirl-pools, steam rooms, and carriage and boat rides. Children can enjoy their own programs in canoeing, swimming, sailing, theater, bowling, and arts and crafts. They even have the unique opportunity to fly on a trapeze.

Whistler Village hosts an impressive array of athletic and cultural events. Sporting activities include golf camps and tournaments, racquetball and tennis championships, and the Cheakamus Challenge—the longest off-road bicycle race in North America.

221

Just south of the resort, Brandywine Falls thunders into its rock basin, plummeting nearly 300 feet.

Concerts on the mountain by the Vancouver Symphony Orchestra, festivals showcasing the magic and merriment of street performers, and major music and folk art fairs are just a few examples of Whistler's cultural celebrations.

At Chateau Whistler itself, cobblestone paths, gabled towers, beamed ceilings, hand-stenciled pecan paneling, and many other fine European influences are blended into the grand design. Modern concern for wastefulness is effectively addressed within the hotel: blue recycling bins are located in all guest rooms and offices; low-flow valves reduce water consumption; old towels are made into rags; and the kitchen uses only chemical- and preservative-free ingredients.

LEANNA RATHKELLY

A wary bobcat (right) watches hikers move along Nairn Falls Trail (above).

Even the lavish gardens are sensitive to their surroundings. Growth is enhanced with organic fertilizers while harmful insects are controlled by natural pest management practices.

In a place so filled with rare and amazing things, one shouldn't be so surprised to discover another rare and amazing thing, the existence of cooperation and restraint. At Whistler, traditionally conflicting interests pull together to uphold the philosophy that we don't leave this world to our children—we borrow it from them.

North of Whistler Village, glacial run-off races through Nairn Falls' chiseled canyons.

Sunset's afterglow on Lost Lake

THE
RESORT
*S*EMIAHMOO

Semiahmoo Bay offers up breathtaking views of its rugged Pacific Coast setting.

When you've gone just about as far north and as far west as you can go and still be in the continental United States, you'll have arrived in Blaine, Washington. Today, this coastal border town is a busy entryway for international traffic, welcoming travelers with its beautifully appointed and maintained Peace Arch State Park. Had you arrived a century or so earlier, you would have witnessed the roots of its seafaring heritage as it bustled with the energy of its prolific salmon fishing and canning operations.

By 1965, the canneries were locked up. The fish were fished out. The only clues left of a once-prosperous industry were the buildings, now filled with echoes and memories of noisy young men boarding the Alaska Packers Association's three-masted "Star" sailing ships for a one-way voyage to the gold fields of Alaska. Drayton Harbor, in 1880, was crowded with fishing boats, ocean freighters, passenger steamers, and various other commercial vessels. In 1980, its waters were shared primarily by recreational water craft, eagles, seals, porpoises, whales, loons, and herons. Positioned north of Puget Sound and the San Juan Islands, the site's ecological abundance was of particular interest to groups such as the Audubon Society.

By 1986, another player had come on board. The 1.5-mile-long sand spit dividing Semiahmoo Bay and Drayton Harbor now boasted an attractive hotel where worn-out canneries had stood; and the adjoining headland now embraced an exclusive golf course and residential development. Could the seemingly incompatible agendas of the Audubon Society and The Resort Semiahmoo find any common ground?

It didn't hurt to ask. The Resort Semiahmoo warranted consideration for the Audubon Cooperative Sanctuary System program. It would be a stellar chance to demonstrate its commitment to environmentally sound maintenance practices and long-term natural resource stewardship.

Even before the Audubon Society's interest, Semiahmoo had earned *Golf Magazine*'s Silver Medal Resort award, and its Arnold Palmer–Ed Seay-designed golf club had been named 1987's "Best New Resort Course" by *Golf Digest*.

Semiahmoo is situated in Whatcom County, two-thirds of which consists of federally regulated forests and parks. North Cascades National Park's wilderness wasn't even accessible by modern roads until 1972.

Sculpted bunkers and tall timber fortify Semiahmoo Golf & Country Club's opening hole.

An entertaining ring-necked duck (below) zigzags across the reflecting pond that separates the 11th (above right side) and 12th (above left side) greens. MIKE KLEMME, GOLFOTO

Appreciation for nature runs high in such a region, which is precisely why the Audubon

proposal was so enticing.

Semiahmoo's directors examined the standards that needed to be met in order to qualify for certification: environmental planning, public involvement and education, water conservation, wildlife habitat management, integrated pest management, and water quality management.

The jagged Coast Mountains accentuate the scenery of the 14th hole.

In 1991, Semiahmoo Golf & Country Club brought its practices into harmony with Audubon guidelines and became one of fewer than fifty golf courses in the country to participate in the exemplary program. The course's policies include: coordinating birdwatching field trips; naturalizing out-of-play areas; and leaving non-hazardous "snag" trees as is. In addition, over 500 native trees were planted; only organic fertilizers are used; drought tolerant grasses are grown; rain water is collected and utilized; turf sprinkling is kept to a minimum; sterile carp help control aquatic weeds; and bat houses and bird-nesting boxes attract the insect-feeding creatures.

Arrowheads (far left)
and buck beans (left)
flourish within the reedy pond
fronting the 6th green (below).

The gently contoured 7,000-yard layout features wide fairways lined by heavy stands of second growth hemlock, fir, cedar, and alder.

An adventurous hooded merganser (below) visits Semiahmoo's 18th hole (above).   COURTESY OF THE RESORT SEMIAHMOO

Free-form ponds and close to sixty white sand bunkers add aesthetic beauty and technical challenge. Paved cart paths and state-of-the-art drainage systems limit weather and traffic damage, keeping the course consistently playable while reducing the need for excessive grooming. Golf can be enjoyed year-round here in this Pacific Northwest destination thanks to the moderating influence of the Strait of Georgia.

The rich woods bordering the 13th hole (above) shelter populations of black-tailed deer (below right) and creeping Oregon grape (below left).

MIKE KLEMME, GOLFOTO

COURTESY OF THE RESORT SEMIAHMOO

In addition to golf, the 1,100-acre resort offers its residents and guests tennis courts, swimming pools, walking paths, and a variety of health club facilities. Greenbelts keep vehicles away from the jogging trails and cycling lanes which climb through majestic firs and wind along pebbled beaches. The resort's five-mile stretch of unspoiled shoreline supports a wonderful array of bird life. Wading birds pick for lunch among the shellfish which thrive in the shallows, while raptors dive for their catches in the bays and coves. The beach is a relaxing spot to comb for such treasures as sand dollars, driftwood, clams, and oysters. A short cruise from the resort, the magnificent San Juan Islands present sightseers with endless opportunities to observe ospreys, Dall's porpoises, harbor seals, bald eagles, and killer and minke whales in their native habitats.

Named for one of the American Indian tribes that originally occupied this territory, Semiahmoo is surrounded by numerous reminders of its extraordinary past.

Semiahmoo's narrow sand spit accommodates the resort's stylish inn (left), hunting bald eagles (above and opposite page top left), and vestiges of salmon packing factories (opposite page top right and bottom).

The skeletal frames of a few of the century-old salmon canneries were even assimilated into the hotel; and the main lobby's grand double-faced fireplace was built with bricks recovered from a cannery's crumbling boiler room.

Near the neck of the spit, one of the former bunkhouses now contains a volunteer-run maritime museum.

234

The spit is also home to families of harbor seals (below) and a weathered representative of the legendary Salmon Gillnetter fleet (above).

The museum's artifacts and artworks highlight not only the fishing industry, but Drayton Harbor's cultural and natural histories as well.

235

The resort's future will also focus on its past. One long-range development plan has earmarked other cannery buildings to be transformed into Lighthouse Square, a festival market village of shops and restaurants.

That recreation for humans and habitat for wildlife can coexist as well as they do at Semiahmoo calls to mind Aldo Leopold's essay on "The Community Concept."

Voyages out of Semiahmoo Marina (below) are periodically joined by majestic killer whales (above).

In this work, the author defines an ideal partnership between people and the planet: "All ethics so far evolved rest upon a single premise: that the individual is a member of a community of interdependent parts...the land simply enlarges the boundaries of the community to include soils, waters, plants and animals...in short, a land ethic changes the role of Homo Sapiens from conqueror of the land to plain member and citizen of it."

Generations later, the writing is still relevant, and its wisdoms are still emulated by organizations such as The Resort Semiahmoo.

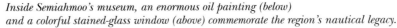

Inside Semiahmoo's museum, an enormous oil painting (below) and a colorful stained-glass window (above) commemorate the region's nautical legacy.

Distant views of British Columbia's mainland are revealed from the lush hilltops of the resort's Boundary Ridge.

Semiahmoo Bay at low tide

*Meadows accented by Canada milkvetch (below left) and
red baneberry (below right) flowers fringe a picturesque inlet along Drayton Harbor (above).*

240

The International Peace Arch honors the long-standing goodwill between Canada and the United States.

Sunset illuminates Semiahmoo Bay.

SUNRIVER RESORT

The life-giving waters of the Deschutes River move lazily over Sunriver's high desert plain.

*I*f you want to gamble on sunshine for your golf vacation, you'll have about a 75 percent chance of success at Sunriver Resort in Oregon, since a typical year produces an average of 265 bright and cloudless days.

So it is in the high desert, where surprisingly, lack of rain does not equate with lack of water. Two rivers—the Deschutes and Little Deschutes—tumble through this hilly country below the volcanic cones of the Cascade Range. The rain that does fall is enough to nourish thickets of juniper, stands of lodgepole and ponderosa pine, and clumps of sagebrush that seem to grow out of bare rock.

Water is also the critical element that helps to sustain the local wildlife, who share these elevations with the human residents. Cougars, bobcats, coyotes, elk, porcupines, river otters, and various species of hawks, owls, and eagles are just some of the amazing creatures who make Sunriver their home.

Eons ago there was much more water here; in fact, the majority of the region was covered by a lake that held fish and gathered game for the Indians who first inhabited this place as long as 15,000 years ago. Sandals made of sagebrush—estimated to be 9,000 years old—were found at Fort Rock Cave, still caked with lakeshore mud; this telling bit of evidence confirmed the existence of the ancient lake.

Eventually, the lake went dry as drought stole away its living abundance. Those who couldn't endure the harsher climate moved on. Those who stayed and persevered are the ancestors of today's tribes: the Paiute, Mono, and Paviotso. They were here to greet the eighteenth-century French fur traders who had doggedly pushed their way across the continent. Being the territory's only white settlers, the French plied their trade in relative peace for many years; but with the trail blazed and the potential for great wealth uncovered, wagon trains and railroads soon followed. Generations earlier, the Indians were able to adapt when lakes became deserts, but most would not survive the drastic changes brought on by livestock ranching, crop farming, and the white man's diseases and alcohol.

244

*The native habitats bordering Sunriver Meadows' 1st hole (above) provide cover
for the course's reclusive badgers (opposite page top) and defiant red-winged blackbirds (opposite page bottom).*

The rush to exploit the land's "endless" riches decimated the indigenous cultures here, just as it had done throughout the New World.

We have learned an especially hard lesson from the mistakes of the past: our planet's reserves are anything but infinite. One of these reserves—wilderness itself—helps to maintain a balance of nature that invisibly supports human life.

ED PARK

We may not understand how all the pieces fit together to realize that balance, but it's important to give them their place in the wheel. People are discovering that Chief Seattle was wise before his time, and knew what he was talking about when he said, "what we do to the Earth, we do to ourselves."

That attitude was adopted by the partners who launched the 3,300-acre Sunriver Resort in the 1960s; and when the organization celebrated its twenty-fifth anniversary in 1993, it pledged that any further development would never undermine the integrity of the natural environment.

SUNRIVER RESORT: CHAPTER 12

At the time of its silver anniversary, Sunriver Resort was already operating two golf courses. Its first course, the aptly named Sunriver Meadows, was conceived by Fred Federspiel in the late '60s.

Sunriver Meadows #13

The Meadows' closing hole (above) edges the course's teeming wetlands (below).

The Meadows' terrain is long and slightly rolling. While fairways and greens are generally open, several mature groves of ponderosa pine tighten up a number of holes.

Sunriver Woodlands is an equally descriptive name for the resort's second golf course.

249

The vast forest backdropping Sunriver Woodlands' 7th hole (above)
conceals a broad array of plants and animals, including pinedrops (opposite page bottom) and porcupines (opposite page top).

250

Sunriver Woodlands #8

Holes at the Woodlands boast such natural defenses as lava rock formations, dark expanses of juniper and pine, and sun-drenched roughs dotted with sagebrush and manzanita. Robert Trent Jones, Jr.'s stellar design rewards players with unforgettable views of the high backcountry that reaches up steadily towards Mt. Bachelor.

Crosswater Club, Sunriver Resort's highly acclaimed third course, was completed in 1995. Architects Robert Cupp and John Fought gracefully worked the site's ranging meadows and pristine forests into their brilliant heathland-style creation. Converging just west of the clubhouse, the Deschutes and Little Deschutes Rivers guard nearly half of Crosswater's holes.

Sunriver Woodlands #18

Cupp and Fought carefully routed their holes around such existing landmarks as mucky bogs, grassy hollows, dry creeks, and even an osprey nest. Furthermore, to help ensure the health and vitality of the course's wetlands, sophisticated drainage and irrigation systems were painstakingly installed. The exquisite 600-acre golf community earned *Golf Digest*'s "Best New Resort Course" award for 1995.

With the opening of Crosswater, the resort proudly assumed the role of environmental protectionist. Many residents and guests attend a series of workshops which teach them to respect the indigenous flora and fauna. To minimize impact damage to sensitive ground vegetation, paved and earthen paths were put down for walkers and cyclists. The Sunriver Nature Center—a private, non-profit corporation—supplements the resort's efforts with interpretive hikes, lectures, and slide shows.

253

The imposing Great Hall (top) is filled with tributes to Sunriver's wild creatures (left) and Western heritage (above).

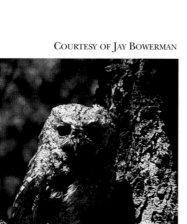

Its botanical garden showcases a number of the area's hardy plant species, and an observatory tracks the sky's constellations. The center's bird rehabilitation program gets people face to face with some of the raptors which hunt and fish in central Oregon's high desert.

The Great Hall is a relic of Camp Abbot, a U.S. Army Corps of Engineers training facility constructed in 1943 on land now owned by Sunriver Resort.

The Sunriver Nature Center entertains visitors with educational exhibits (above right), astronomy demonstrations (right), and occasional sightings of flammulated owls (above center) and American kestrels (above left).

The Sunriver Nature Center is situated close to the Deschutes River and its adjoining marshes (above) and shallows (below).

More than 500 massive pine logs were brought in to build the former officers club; and nearly 160 cubic yards of stone were needed to complete its two grand fireplaces. Today, the versatile structure hosts a multitude of conventions, receptions, dinners, dances, and music festivals. The Great Hall has retained its original rustic character while keeping pace with the times: high-speed telecommunications data lines enable guests to access the world with just a few keystrokes.

Sporting challenges abound at Sunriver. To complement its fifty-four holes of golf, the resort maintains twenty-eight tennis courts, two swimming pools, thirty-five miles of paved cycling paths, horse stables, and an indoor racquet club.

North of the resort,
the High Desert Museum honors central Oregon's fascinating past.

Dwarf purple monkey flowers (below left) and common blue-eyed grass (below right) flourish on the margins of Crosswater's 13th hole (above).   COURTESY OF DOST & EVANS, FOCUS ON GOL

Positioned within the Deschutes National Forest, Sunriver Resort is surrounded by plenty of fresh-air recreational opportunities. The Deschutes River, the area's premier attraction, is a designated wild and scenic waterway that lures serious whitewater rafters and kayakers. Fishing and canoeing are two popular diversions at the resort, which embraces a quieter section of the treasured river.

COURTESY OF JAY BOWERMAN

Located just east of the resort, the Newberry National Volcanic Monument encompasses several not-yet-extinct volcanoes and their ancient lava flows, including a sizeable obsidian tube (a volcanic glass) which the Native Americans chipped to fashion sharp tools and weapons. Hikers can even trek to an "animal inn" to study the peculiar behaviors of various cavity-dwelling creatures; and to Newberry's closely protected cache of pumice grape-fern (which grows in only three other zones in North America).

A few miles from Newberry, the High Desert Museum's 150 acres of world-class indoor and outdoor displays commemorate the region's distinctive natural and cultural histories.

Man and nature's forces merge flawlessly at Crosswater's dynamic 12th hole.

Sunriver Resort long ago recognized the importance of teaching youngsters about the Earth's ecology, and for many years it has been doing just that. Ponds, fish, wolves, and raptors are just a few of the subjects addressed by classes and camps tailored exclusively for children.

Managed by Destination Hotels and Resorts, Sunriver Resort is dedicated to perpetuating an upscale quality of life for humans that doesn't significantly disturb the existing plant and animal communities. To help promote this objective, the resort has published a booklet for residents entitled, *Living With Wildlife: A Field Guide to Living at Crosswater*. It introduces local flora and fauna, describes their needs, and then suggests ways these needs can be satisfied.

Crosswater's sprawling grounds are highlighted by hunting coyotes (below) and nesting ospreys (above).

The exhilarating scenery of the high desert engulfs Crosswater's 10th (below) and 18th (above) holes.

Lava Lands Visitor Center invites explorations of Lava Butte's craggy base (opposite page top) and primeval flows (above).

A juvenile turkey vulture (below left) and a twisted ponderosa pine (right) enliven Lava Cast Forest's stark terrain.

Recommendations include using building materials that are friendly to the environment; customizing feeding stations for specific mammals and birds; and growing trees, shrubs, and herbaceous plants which provide wildlife with sources of food and habitat.

263

Lava Cast's rugged flows (above) are ideal sanctuaries for colonies of great horned owls (top left and right).

The footpath overlooking the turbulent waters of Benham Falls (above) winds alongside clusters of arrowleaf balsamroot (far left) and giant red paintbrush (left).

264

SUNRIVER RESORT: CHAPTER 12

Striving to safeguard Sunriver Resort's pure setting, the manual even discusses such diverse matters as catch-and-release fishing and the control of pets.

Homeowners are urged to learn as much as they can about their lots before making changes, because replacing destroyed native growth is far more difficult than preserving it in the first place. Since visitors and residents wish to experience Sunriver as an unspoiled property, they eagerly accept their role of responsibility and do their part to keep it unspoiled.

At day's end, Sunriver's magnificent bobcats patrol the wooded trails.

Sundown over the Cascade Range reflects off a scenic bend in the Deschutes River.

THE INN AND LINKS
AT
SPANISH BAY™

Just south of the resort, Point Joe engages the ocean's powerful surge.

Long-term preservation of the land and the short-sighted desires of those who wish to utilize the land are, by nature, at odds. Stories are common about people who construct homes in the woods and then cut down trees to open up the view; or people who choose to live on a lake so they can enjoy the wildlife, and then spray to eliminate the insects which help to sustain the wildlife.

Every day, golf courses stare into the horns of that dilemma. They are expected to maintain neatly clipped expanses of lush, flawless perfection; yet to realize that perfection often requires adopting practices which ultimately endangers it.

This was just one of the important issues addressed at the high-profile conference "Golf and the Environment: Charting a Sustainable Future," hosted by *The Inn at Spanish Bay* in 1995. In selecting the venue for the discussions, the Center for Resource Management Company, *Golf Digest* magazine, and the National Wildlife Federation couldn't have chosen a more ecologically sound ally.

The Inn and Links at Spanish Bay, a *Golf Magazine* Gold Medal Resort, was built by Pebble Beach Company on California's fabled Monterey Peninsula. Beginning in the early 1900s, the acreage the resort now occupies was extensively mined for the white sand that would replenish Hawaii's beaches and be used as a component in glass-making operations. By 1973, the original dunes and vegetation were all but lost, and many of the area's creatures had long since moved on in search of other food sources. The ravaged landscape desperately needed mending.

Because Pebble Beach Company was already looking after the peninsula's fragile habitats—employing a full-time forester, ecologist, and nursery manager—the monumental task of bringing the dunes back became its number one priority.

The Links at Spanish Bay #2

To begin the process, over 500,000 cubic yards of sandy fill were moved to the location by conveyor belts, formed into high mounds, and then layered with a broad array of compatible coastal plants. To further dress the young dunes, seed was gathered on site and propagated inside Pebble Beach Company's greenhouses. Invasive non-native species—such as French broom, ice plant, and pampas grass—were systematically eradicated.

The remnant dune flanking the right side of the 9th hole (below) is enriched by clumps of seaside daisies (above right) and endangered Menzie's wallflowers (above left).

The naturalized margins of the par-three 4th hole (above) are havens for the course's black-tailed deer (below and opposite page).

Finally, boardwalks were put down to accommodate foot and wheelchair traffic over the delicate, revegetated surfaces.

Achieving environmental integrity at *Spanish Bay*, however, required more than just dune restoration. A valuable coastal marsh and the neighboring Del Monte Forest were also exhaustively regenerated by Pebble Beach Company's employees. With so much attention devoted to the area, it's again possible to share the scenery with fishing gulls, cormorants, and pelicans; and to stroll along the ocean watching for playful gray whales, sea lions, sea otters, and harbor seals. In fact, scores of harbor seals return to the coastline each spring to have their pups. Gene Fryberger—Pebble Beach Company's ecologist—and his crew erect signage and fencing to help safeguard the seals. Once the pups are born, company personnel carefully monitor the progress of the gentle creatures.

In addition, Pebble Beach Company has participated in a $34 million, privately funded co-operative venture to install modified water pumping stations and water treatment and storage reservoirs. These facilities reclaim wastewater for irrigating the golf courses and athletic fields within Del Monte Forest, conserving potable water for more vital needs, such as human consumption. The company also administers highly successful glass, paper, plastic, aluminum, battery, and motor and cooking oil recycling plans. About 2,500 tons of green waste from forestry and golf course operations are composted each year; and educational outreach programs and guided field trips teach people to recognize and appreciate the peninsula's wild abundance.

274

Healthy groupings of pink sand verbena (above),
Tidestrom's lupine (right), Indian paintbrush (top right),
and silvery California sagewort (top right)
texture and stabilize the rejuvenated dunes
alongside Spanish Bay's 3rd hole (opposite page).

The par-three 8th and its thriving coastal marsh

Following the theory that responsible land management practices can perpetuate the existence and enjoyment of golf, *The Links at Spanish Bay* has significantly reduced the risk of chemical contamination by minimizing fertilizer and pesticide applications. A great deal of the layout is ungroomed or only lightly manicured, allowing its raw character to dominate the look and challenge—much like the legendary designs of Scotland, where the game continues to be immensely popular even though its courses are less poshly upholstered.

From the outset, the windswept masterpiece has been showered with accolades from such respected publications as *Golf Digest* (1988 "Best New Resort Course"), *Condé Nast Traveler* (1996 "Number One Mainland Resort"), and *Meetings & Conventions* (1997 "Gold Tee" award). Furthermore, *The Links at Spanish Bay* was honored with 1994's prestigious "National Environmental Steward Award" from the Golf Course Superintendents Association of America.

The spectacular linksland-style creation was born out of an alliance that blended the imaginations of three of golf's foremost personalities—Robert Trent Jones, Jr., Tom Watson, and Frank "Sandy" Tatum.

This section of California has long been of interest to botanists. As early as 1785, collecting expeditions from France named and catalogued the tremendous variety of trees, shrubs, and herbaceous plants which flourish here.

The pristine Monterey pine forest confining the 10th hole (below) is home to a colony of western fence lizards (above).

The resort's boardwalks present hikers with interpretive signage (above left), stunning panoramas of the Pacific shore (above right), and unique perspectives of the 17th hole (below).

Gene Fryberger proudly shows off the
unusual flora of the S.F.B. Morse Botanical Reserve (above).

Centuries before that, the Costanoan Indians relied on the plants for food and medicine. Shaggybark manzanita alleviated poison oak rashes; Christmas berry bark teas cured stomach-aches; and horsetail was ingested to treat kidney disorders.

Live oak acorns were made into bread and porridge; chamise was applied to skin infections; and poison oak oil was needed to bake bread and weave baskets. Bear grass, which only flowers after a fire, helped to waterproof the baskets.

Trail guides from the
Pebble Beach Equestrian
Center conduct horseback
tours of the peninsula's
treasured hillsides (above right)
and beaches (right).

In 1984, an archeological site was established at *Spanish Bay*. The discoveries of relic mortars and pestles, hearth stones, arrowheads, scrapers, and shell and bone fragments hinted at what life was like for the natives prior to the arrival of the Spanish in 1769. Settlement by the Europeans doomed the Costanoan Indians, who were annihilated by introduced diseases against which they had no immunity.

By 1850, California was a state, and Monterey Bay was famous for its Chinese fishermen and the dazzling abalone shells they retrieved from the ocean floor.

A weary sea lion (above) stretches over the rocks of a churning inlet near Spanish Bay (below).

Roxayne Spruance, Pebble Beach Company's naturalist (above), surveys Fanshell Beach and its vigorous kelp beds (below right) and feeding black-necked stilts (below left).

Between 1850 and 1885, Portuguese and New England sailors recklessly hunted the region's migrating whales to the brink of extinction. Later, the sardine fishing and canning industries brought prosperity to the idyllic seaside town of Monterey. Although the sardines were virtually fished out and the canneries mainly closed down by the 1940s, memories of that era live on, thanks in part to the enduring works of John Steinbeck, the celebrated American novelist who spent several years in the Monterey area. Today, the bay's calamari catch is widely regarded as North America's most appetizing.

COURTESY OF JANICE HOPKINS-SNABLY

Day's last light glows across the Lone Cypress (below) and Pescadero Point (above), two exhilarating stops on 17-Mile Drive.

As much as it was utilized for its natural resources, the peninsula was just as valued for its natural beauty. Samuel F.B. Morse, great-grand-nephew of the telegraph inventor, disagreed with proposals to divide up a portion of Del Monte Forest for residences, suggesting instead it be transformed into a championship golf course.

High trails at Point Lobos State Reserve offer up bracing views of Headland Cove (above) and Weston Beach (below).

Being a man of remarkable vision, Morse reasoned that sensitive tracts of land might be better protected if left whole and conscientiously managed for a single, low-impact purpose. *The Lodge at Pebble Beach* was completed in 1909, and *Pebble Beach Golf Links* was ready for play by 1919.

Wanting to restrict commercial expansion, Morse then bought up the balance of Del Monte Forest adjacent to *Pebble Beach*. He eventually sold generous parcels of unspoiled oceanfront property to the town of Pacific Grove after its councilors promised that the parcels would remain unspoiled.

In 1971, the S.F.B. Morse Botanical Reserve was dedicated to commemorate Pebble Beach Company's distinguished founder. Situated inside Del Monte Forest, the eighty-four-acre allotment of rare flora is avidly hiked and studied by scientists and sightseers from around the world.

China Cove (below) is a favorite sanctuary for Point Lobos' harbor seals (above).

Three thousand of Del Monte's 5,200 acres are permanently shielded from development. It is the only place on Earth where Bishop and Monterey pine grow side by side; and where Gowan cypress and Bishop pine survive in the poor, acidic soil as pygmies, attaining heights of only three to ten feet.

Pacific Grove is highlighted by such architectural gems as the Point Pinos Light Station (top), the Green Gables Inn (center), and the Centrella Hotel (bottom).

The breathtaking sights and sounds of *17-Mile Drive* (one of only nine private tollroads in the country) have been thrilling travelers for more than a century. Each year, about 1.5 million people explore the roadway's glorious uplands, valleys, seashore, cliffs, and coves. At designated turnouts on the winding loop, Pebble Beach Company's ecologists enhance the experience with intriguing natural history lessons.

284

Monterey's Fisherman's Wharf (above) and a resident brown pelican (below)

The *Lone Cypress*, one of the most recognizable landmarks on *17-Mile Drive*, clings tenaciously to the top of a jagged rock promontory. Perched just above the ocean's pounding surf, the beloved sentinel is estimated to have stood watch here for well over 200 years.

Down the coast from *Spanish Bay*, Point Lobos State Reserve provides people with yet another opportunity to commune with nature. Its 554 acres of rugged headlands, secluded inlets, and grassy meadows nurture up to 350 different plant and 250 different animal species.

In 1960, the nation's first underwater park was created when 750 submerged acres were annexed to the state land.

Staff from *The Inn at Spanish Bay* encourage visitors to sign up for the resort's "Ansel Adams Camera Walks." Led by a naturalist and a professional photographer, these outings may appear to be designed only for the entertainment of guests, but they do, in fact, promote greater awareness of our environment.

At the Monterey Bay Aquarium, Roxayne Spruance helps to raise an orphaned sea otter pup (above and below).

When one's view of the planet is narrowed to that which can be seen through the lens, understanding dawns: everything is a singular, precisely fitted thread in a larger weaving. To care for little things—such as the insects—reinforces the larger fabric of life.

Historic Cotton Hall (below) and Custom House (above) have graced the streets of Monterey since the first half of the nineteenth century.

The sun sets brilliantly alongside Monterey Peninsula's weathered crags and coves.

THE
ℬOULDERS

Sunrise silhouettes the resort's breathtaking desert terrain.

So artfully does the sidewinder rattlesnake move, that only two small points of contact exist between its long, slender body and the scorching Arizona sand; scarcely any track bears evidence to its having been there. So skillfully was The Boulders blended with the desert that man seems to leave little more trace than the snake.

Golf usually conjures up lush, green images of impeccably manicured fairways and putting surfaces. Here in the high Sonoran desert, however, it is played as much over wild expanses as it is over groomed turfgrass. Towering eucalyptus and palm trees are nowhere to be seen. Instead, 300-year-old saguaro cactus lend native touches of vegetation to this spectacular setting.

As its name suggests, primeval granite heaps are the most unusual features of this most unusual place. The Boulders is located at Carefree, Arizona, and indeed, the rock fragments might have been strewn about like a carefree giant's toys on the playroom floor. They were, in fact, thrust up out of the Earth's bedrock eons ago when the San Andreas fault shifted and formed several "fault block" mountain chains throughout North America.

During the next 12 million years, rain eroded the blocks of granite into rounded boulders, and wind shaped them into balancing rocks. Amid dozens of such natural sculptures lies Black Mountain, The Boulders' reigning landmark. Rising 3,400 feet above sea level, its dramatically tapered and colored peaks have been admired by explorers for approximately 11,000 years now.

The Desert Archaics, a nomadic tribe who passed through in about 9000 B.C., were the first people to see this imposing landscape. By A.D. 1, a race from Meso-America had found their way north, bringing with them knowledge of agriculture and irrigation. The Hohokam built an elaborate 500-mile canal system to carry water from faraway rivers to their terraced fields; but even the most sophisticated canals couldn't deliver enough water to fend off the thirty-year drought that parched the area during the twelfth century.

The par-three 3rd hole at Boulders South

Not able to endure the killing drought, the Hohokam abandoned their villages of thatch-and-mud pit houses, leaving behind the woven tapestries, etched seashells, and twill and lace work which have provided archeologists with valuable clues as to what life was like for this early civilization.

The South's 5th green rests below the resort's premier boulder formation.

The next visitors were Athapaskan nomads, who hunted and gathered here during their migration from the north, but left little to tell of their sojourns. The sixteenth-century residents, however, were not so unobtrusive. The Spanish influence reached up into the Arizona desert as colonists brought grain, metal, and livestock to wring productivity from the arid soil. Missionaries followed, attempting to wring pagan beliefs from the natives.

Boulders South #7

The hole's teeboxes feature a massive, tilted boulder (above left),
colorful northern cardinals (top right) and roosting white-winged doves (above right).

Foremost among the missionaries was the Italian priest, Father Kino, who traveled extensively in the late 1600s, mapping and teaching across present-day Arizona.

This era also witnessed the introduction of firearms to the region. Besides employing them for hunting and protection, the Spanish would all too often wield their deadly weapons to greedily take what wasn't theirs to take. Written accounts of the fierce, bloody clashes between the Europeans and the Apache recall a truly dark period of American history.

When gold fever struck the United States in the 1800s, a feverish influx of people moved west to search for the riches which—according to the dime novels—lay there for the taking. With their heads full of romantic tales about unclaimed wealth and unoccupied land, the pioneers trespassed against the Indians; once again, the restless frontier was ravaged by violence.

The U.S. Army established forts and sent troops, more settlers arrived with their wagons and dreams, and by 1889, the bustling territory had elected Phoenix as its capital. Twenty-three years later, Arizona became the country's forty-eighth state.

Boulders South #8

Land use continued to be the overriding issue for the state. As new channels, lakes, and dams were constructed, new commercial ventures were launched. Tragically, one of these fledgling operations would trigger more hostilities. The Pleasant Valley War, a bitter feud between opposing sheep and cattle ranchers, plagued Arizona for over five years.

With the onset of World War II, Phoenix was converted into a busy training center for the armed forces. Military installations lingered after the war, but many of the returning men and women in uniform re-entered private life and initiated peacetime businesses. The growing population required more water, so several additional dams were built to collect the flow of this highly treasured resource.

Lively cactus wrens (opposite page top), thickets of chainfruit cholla (above), blooming claret-cup cactus (bottom left), and fruiting barrel cactus (bottom right) animate the hole's transitional zones.

The rocks and desert scrub flanking the South course's 10th hole (above)
are home to greater roadrunners (opposite page bottom left), Gambel's quail (opposite page bottom right), and black-chinned hummingbirds (opposite page top).

With the advent of air conditioning, the desert's appeal spread to a whole new generation of adventurers. Tourists came to visit dude ranches, sampled the relaxed Western lifestyle, and decided to stay. Carefree, founded by K.T. Palmer and Tom Darlington, blossomed into one of central Arizona's most desirable communities, enticing retirees and celebrities with its laid-back, comfortable atmosphere.

In the 1970s, conservational attitudes became interwoven with developmental pressures. When Rusty Lyon transformed 1,300 acres on the outskirts of Carefree into The Boulders, he stated, "We shared a single vision: to create an exhilarating desert place, a landscape where man-made architecture would be subordinate to the natural environment...we pledged never to compromise the integrity of the desert."

The distinction between sand and turf is sharply defined at the South's par-three 15th hole (above and opposite page).

And neither did the desert compromise the integrity of The Boulders, which is repeatedly presented with *Golf Magazine*'s Gold Medal Resort award. Project architect Bob Bacon accepted the design task as a biologist, not as an engineer. Honoring Native American practices, his first priority was to utilize what Mother Earth had supplied. Bacon even lived on site for fifteen months to gain a better understanding of the land and its fragile ecosystems.

To spare the desert floor from excessive scraping, Bacon vigilantly build around most of the resort's mature trees, shrubs, and cactus. If plants had to be moved, they were held in a nursery and replanted once construction was complete. Finally, to complement the property's indigenous vegetation, botanists researched and imported exotic species from Australia and South Africa.

The development fits easily into its desert surroundings. Utilities are buried out of sight, structures are colored to match the sand, and walls are hand-plastered to give them an organic texture (sharp edges simply do not exist). Cactus wrens and Gila woodpeckers visit alfresco dining patios to beg for handouts, while coyotes and roadrunners frequent golf course arroyos to hunt for prey.

The Boulders' well-appointed main lodge was styled to mimic its craggy backdrop.

Jay Morrish was commissioned to design the Boulders North and Boulders South golf courses, an assignment that was carried out in three separate stages between 1981 and 1991. Respecting the resort's wishes and the ecologists' regulations, Morrish carefully positioned his fairways, teeboxes, and putting surfaces (the golf courses' only green belts) into the unspoiled terrain.

*Interpretive walks of the Boulders Trail are
conducted by Jeff Hayes, the resort's horticulturalist.*

With the high desert in play at every hole, scenery throughout is stunning. A graceful old saguaro stands in the middle of a gaping sand trap; an enormous balancing rock and its resident turkey vulture watch over the same hole; and a spiral staircase is carved into the boulder that grants access to a neighboring teebox. And even deserts have their oases: reflective lakes and trickling brooks accentuate both the challenge and the beauty of the two exquisite layouts.

A variety of creatures run through the courses: roadrunners, javelinas, jackrabbits, and kangaroo rats in particular. The resort recommends waving goodbye to errant golf balls; retrieving them can be dangerous, as rattlesnakes, scorpions, and Gila monsters occasionally patrol the courses' rugged boundaries. Even certain cactus should be given wide berth: some believe the chainfruit or "jumping" cholla actually attacks victims who come too close.

Prairie evening-primroses (top left), black-spined prickly pear cactus (top right), and blue palo verde trees (above) help to dress up the resort's grounds.

Nearly all desert plants, though, are quite friendly and remarkably resilient. The palo verde is a mostly leafless tree that photosynthesizes sunlight through its green bark. The creosote bush radiates its roots deep into the sand to locate precious water; incredibly, it even generates different sets of leaves to adapt to varying degrees of moisture in the air. The night-blooming cereus emits a powerful fragrance to attract the moths and butterflies which can't tolerate the heat of day.

The Boulders Trail spans deep ravines (above), passes through granite tunnels (bottom right), reveals prehistoric Indian pestle impressions (bottom left), and explores naturally sculpted and stacked rock formations (opposite page top and bottom).

The desert also provides nourishment. Some locals still harvest the uniquely flavored fruits of prickly pear cactus, mesquite trees, jojoba bushes, and saguaro cactus.

The Boulders is a short drive away from a number of exclusive historical sites. The Montezuma Castle and Casa Grande National Monuments exhibit the ruins of ancient Indian villages; the Superstition Mountains are combed by prospectors hoping to find the legendary Lost Dutchman Gold Mine; and a selection of once-productive gold mines now serve as interpretive centers for curious visitors.

At the resort itself, recreational opportunities range from tennis, swimming, and golf to horseback trips, desert jeep tours, and hot-air balloon rides. In addition, Jeff Hayes hikes guests up to a 400-foot-high rock precipice, where they can survey the vast, untamed landscapes of the Tonto National Forest.

The weathered saguaro cactus of the Boulders Trail (below) house the resort's Gila woodpeckers (above).

Aldo Leopold could have been referring to The Boulders when he wrote in his *Sand County Almanac*, "No one can weigh or measure culture...suffice it to say that by common consent of thinking people, there are cultural values in the sports, customs and experiences that renew contacts with wild things."

Bullock's orioles (above left), chuckwallas (below), and Gila monsters (above right) are just a few of the trail's native inhabitants.

306

Arroyos fronting the North course's 13th (top) and 8th (opposite page bottom) greens feed the resort's javelinas (right and opposite page top).

Boulders North #3

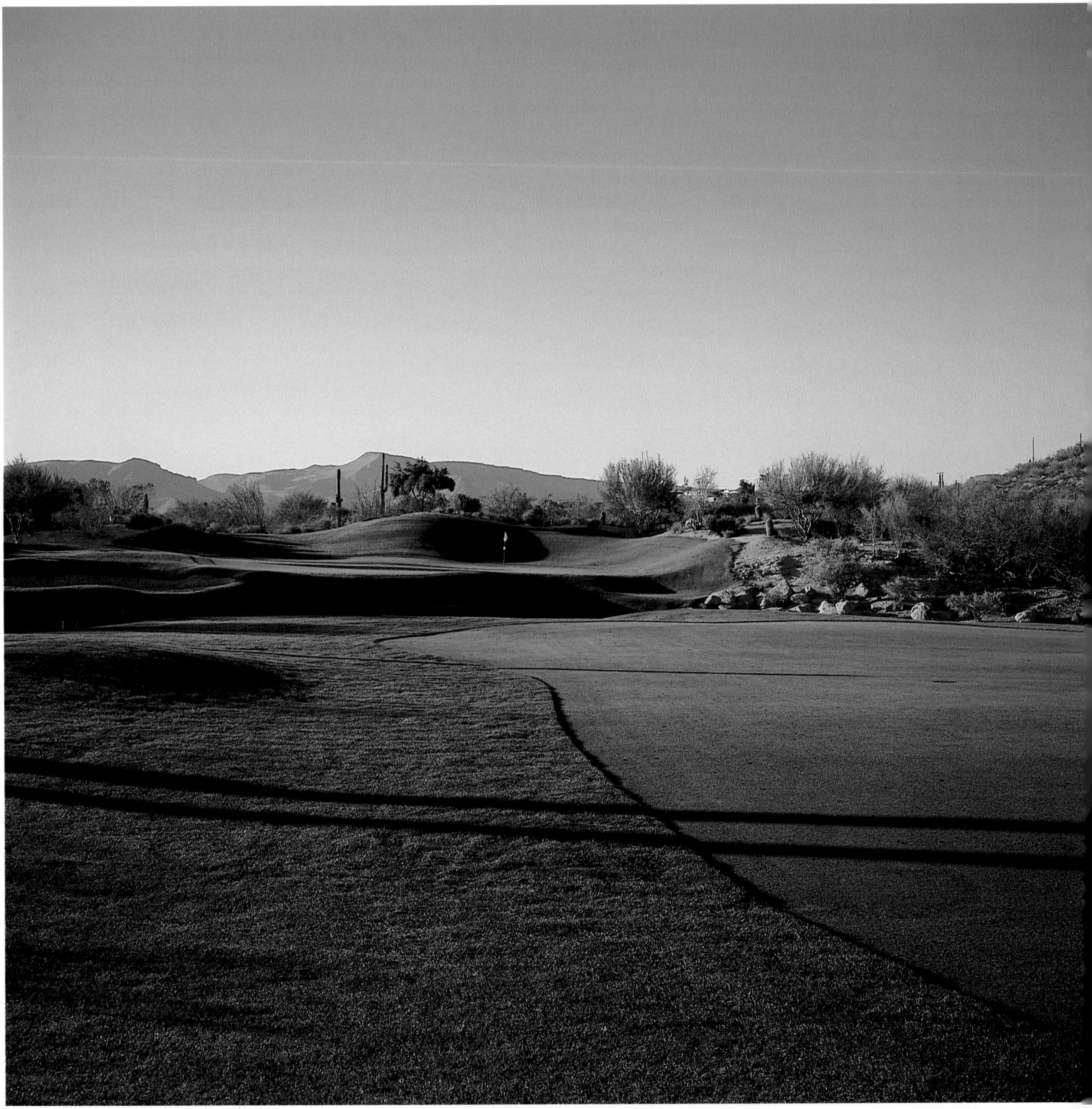

Sundown paints The Boulders' desert sky.

KIAWAH ISLAND
RESORT

Sunrise shimmers on Kiawah Island's outer banks.

Thousands of years before the written history of this continent, tribes of coastal Indians hunted and fished the marshes, forests, and waters of the barrier islands near what we now call South Carolina. They gathered in villages of round and rectangular dwellings encircled by gardens which grew corn, pumpkins, and melons to supplement their diet of fish and game. The oldest recovered pottery in North America is traced to this civilization: the Etiwan, Stono, Bohicket, Wando, and Kiawah.

These were the nations that greeted the French, Spanish, and English explorers of the seventeenth century. They accepted and fed the strangers who otherwise would not have endured the rigors of existence in an unfamiliar country. A most hospitable people, the Kiawah even invited the British to start up the settlement of Charles Town in 1670. By the next century, the tiny colony had evolved into a full-fledged city, and in 1783, it was renamed Charleston.

Once a tribe of about 4,000, disease and slavery introduced by the Europeans quickly decimated the Kiawah Nation. Only a dozen Indians were counted in 1740. Today, little more than place names bear evidence of a culture that had flourished for 10,000 years.

With no natives left to lay claim to the land, ownership was transferred to the new citizens of the New World. In 1699, the Lord's Proprietors deeded Kiawah Island to George Raynor. Mystery has always surrounded Raynor's origin; even the spelling of his name is disputed. Some believe he purchased the land with the spoils of his career as a pirate during the days of Captain Kidd. Others speculate he was granted the land after promising to give up his plundering ways.

Perhaps it was the lure of home and family that drew Raynor away from the danger and adventure of the sea. We know he had a daughter, Mary; we also know she acquired the island following her father's death, and in turn left it to her husband, Roger Moore.

Kiawah's spectacular live oaks and sandy barrens defend The Ocean Course's 1st (above) and 2nd (opposite page) holes.

Life in the Lowcountry apparently didn't suit Moore; the property was sold to John Stanyarne in 1719 or 1737—the records aren't clear on the date.

Stanyarne recognized the island's agricultural potential, and with the labor of nearly 300 slaves to support his endeavors, he developed a lucrative trade in indigo. The plant was highly valued as a fabric dye, and the quality of Kiawah Island's crop was famous. Befitting a man of his position, Stanyarne erected a splendid mansion of cypress and pine with a brick foundation held together by a mortar made from sand and oyster shell lime.

The Ocean Course #4

Stanyarne's granddaughter, Elizabeth Vanderhorst, inherited his holdings in 1772. Her husband, Arnoldus Vanderhorst II, hailed from a colorful and celebrated Charleston family. He was a prominent member of the colonial militia, and twice served as mayor of Charleston and once as governor of South Carolina.

A revitalized marsh creek (above) flows quietly alongside The Ocean Course's 13th hole (below).

Stanyarne's home became the Vanderhorst House, and would accommodate four generations of Vanderhorsts over the next 180 years. It would even host British Revolutionary War troops and be used as a base for the soldiers who guarded Charleston during the Civil War. In fact, the mansion's interior still contains the graffiti scrawled by Union forces in the early 1860s.

The Ocean Course's par-three 14th blends seamlessly into its coastal setting.

Arnoldus IV survived his tour of duty in the Civil War, returned home with his former slaves, and began operating the plantation again—only to be killed in a hunting accident. In his lifetime, the Southern gentleman co-founded the College of Charleston, directed one of the nation's first orphanages, and helped to repeal a number of severe penal codes. Legend has it that on clear, moonlit nights his ghost can still be spotted roaming the island.

Arnoldus V attempted to maintain the plantation's productivity, which under his father's control had yielded generous crops of rice and cotton in addition to indigo. Nature, however, would doom the attempt. Hurricanes and boll weevils destroyed the profitable industry the Vanderhorsts had nurtured for nearly two centuries.

The 17th at The Ocean Course is widely regarded as one of the game's finest par-three holes.

Kiawah Island's staff of biologists conduct ocean seining (above)
and marsh creek canoeing (below) programs for residents and resort guests.

The house was left to occasional use by hunting and fishing parties, and was stripped by thieves of most of its furnishings. Gardens and fields which once featured an exotic variety of fruits, herbs, flowers, and cash crops were gradually reclaimed by the island's indigenous vegetation.

Despite the plagues of nature and time, the venerable old mansion and its traditional Lowcountry staircase remained basically sound. This precious historical artifact was restored in 1995 along with the grand allée of oaks the Vanderhorsts had planted from the yard to the shore.

In 1951, lumberman C.C. Royal paid $125,000 for the overgrown 10,000-acre retreat. During the ensuing two decades he cleared much of the virgin pine forest and second growth timber, built a bridge to connect the island with the mainland, and then sold the acreage for $17 million.

Quieter canoeists are likely to sight
great egrets fishing along a creek's banks.

The year was 1974, and the country's environmental concern was beginning to awaken. Kiawah Island Company's intention was to transform their purchase into a world-class resort and residential property—but not before an exhaustive site analysis was completed. Led by Charles Fraser, a visionary for Southern resort communities, a multidisciplinary task force took sixteen months to prepare a 700-page report that detailed the complex interrelationships between all known ecosystems. The most intensive study ever done of a privately held island, it includes findings on everything from prehistoric man to microscopic phytoplankton.

Great blue herons (top) and snowy egrets (above) are familiar visitors to the resort.

320

Liz King, Kiawah's head naturalist, shows off a pair of the island's reptiles.

Kiawah's unspoiled dunes (top) are inhabited
by elusive ghost crabs (above) and delicate beach morning-glories (opposite page bottom).

The resort was carefully constructed over a four-year period, and in 1978, Kiawah Island was opened to the public. The company's work to preserve the natural treasures of the Lowcountry was honored with the American Society of Landscape Architects' "National Merit Award" and the South Carolina Wildlife Federation's "Conservationist of the Year" distinction.

The island's forty-five square miles are blessed with some sixty-five ponds and lagoons, the Kiawah and Stono Rivers, the Intracoastal Waterway, and tremendous populations of birds, mammals, reptiles, and amphibians.

Kiawah Island Resort has joined with the University of South Carolina to care for the endangered Atlantic loggerhead sea turtles who come to shore at night to lay their eggs.

The resort's leisure trails skirt the island's thriving lagoons and maritime forests.

A trail's edge is enriched by thickets of beauty-berry (above left) and trumpet vine (above right).

Because there are so few remaining nesting grounds, the entire island participates in the ambitious undertaking. Loggerheads are sensitive to light, so people in rooms with windows facing the sea close their curtains after dark to avoid frightening the creatures back into the surf. To prevent the eggs from becoming breakfast for hungry raccoons and herons, biologists transfer the nests to incubation shelters. In the project's first five years, 7,500 hatchlings were released into the ocean, an effort that earned the Isaac Walton League's "National Conservation Award."

Kiawah's plants are as varied as its animals. Forests consist of oak, palmetto, and pine, with a subcanopy of hickory, sweetgum, and magnolia. Red bay, sassafras, wax myrtle, and yaupon dominate the understory, and sea oats cover the sand dunes.

These fragile resources are utilized by the resort's naturalists and marine biologists to encourage others to learn more about their surroundings. In support of this mission, personnel from the Heron Park Center coordinate beach walks; birding excursions; snake, turtle, and alligator explorations; and marsh creek canoeing and kayaking tours.

Other footpaths traverse Kiawah's twisted live oaks and sweeping marshlands.

Hikes through the resort's subtropical forests are frequently joined by wood storks (above) and black-crowned night-herons (below).

Unlike most islands, Kiawah is swelling rather than shrinking. The bulk of the island was formed during the last 4,000 years, but a heavy accretion has occurred since 1896, the year the Charleston Harbor jetties were built. The jetties diverted the southward drift of sediments away from Folly and Morris Islands and their series of shoals. With no shoals left to buffer them against the relentless waves, Folly and Morris have been eroding at an accelerated rate and their sediments have been reinforcing Kiawah's broad beaches.

Four island golf courses—positioned to show off the resort's premier landscapes—present guests with an amazing variety of choices.

Early in 1995, the Marsh Point course was closed and a major renovation project was launched. Reopened in the fall of 1996 as Cougar Point, the Gary Player layout encompasses the Kiawah River and its teeming marshland, where heron, egret, and osprey hunt against a backdrop of needle rush and spartina grass.

Named for the island's nesting loggerhead sea turtles, Turtle Point was officially dedicated by its renowned designer in 1981. Jack Nicklaus shrewdly arranged the holes around such available features as mammoth dunes, vigorous woods, an active pelican rookery, and an alligator-patrolled lake.

At dusk, a wood stork returns to its treetop roost.

To comply with a multitude of environmental restrictions and guidelines, Osprey Point needed to be meticulously planned out long before construction could begin. Completed in 1988, the stellar Tom Fazio creation maneuvers past marshes of cattail and dog fennel, and through forests of pine, palmetto, oak, and magnolia. Four sparkling lakes provide hazards for golfers and habitat for some of the 190 species of island birds.

Conceived by Pete Dye, The Ocean Course opened in May of 1991 (and hosted the Ryder Cup later that very same year). Set on a pristine 2.5-mile-long ribbon of dunes between Kiawah's breezy seacoast and sheltered tidal marshes, the glorious terrain is entirely free of residential and commercial real estate.

Cougar Point's 2nd (below) and 5th (above) holes are highlighted by tightly defended putting surfaces.

Cougar Point #17

COURTESY OF KIAWAH ISLAND RESORT

Turtle Point's 13th hole

With so many extraordinary challenges in the midst of so much natural beauty, The Ocean Course is universally praised as a marvel of modern engineering.

Under the protective glare of its parent (right),
a juvenile alligator (above) suns itself beside a pond at Turtle Point.

*Turtle Point's par-three 16th is naturally enhanced by
panoramic ocean views (above) and hardy clumps of seashore mallow (below).*

Every possible effort was made to integrate the holes with the existing wild abundance. Rather than hauling in soil to contour the playing field, Dye instead used the sand excavated from other sections of the course. To stabilize newly sculpted mounds, he ordered plantings of native sea oats, American beach grass, panic grass, and sweet grass.

Teeshots at Osprey Point's 3rd hole must carry an intimidating expanse of marshland.

The Ocean Course was deliberately routed so that the adjacent wetlands would not be compromised. Dye also installed a sophisticated drainage system to recycle nutrient-rich irrigation water rather than allowing it to run off. He even rescued two saltwater lagoons that had deteriorated after their brackish flows were blocked by the lumbering dikes built in the 1950s.

Within the mire, a decaying snag nourishes a young pine.

Months of painstaking work re-established their original flows and vegetation, and before long, the resurrected lagoons were once again filled with local bird and aquatic life.

In addition to its golf facilities, Kiawah Island Resort maintains ten miles of packed beach for biking and land-sailing; sixteen miles of paved bike paths; and a twenty-one-acre play area for children. Kamp Kiawah also keeps youngsters entertained with events such as "Pirate Escapades" and "Nature Adventure Days."

Outdoor concerts, cookouts, and square dancing enhance the island experience, as do trips to the Straw Market to shop for sweet grass baskets and other unique Lowcountry collectables.

Spikes of pickerelweed (above left) and Spanish bayonet (above right) bloom on the boggy margins.

*The scenic pond on Osprey Point's
par-three 11th hole (left) is an important
fishery for the course's tricolored
herons (top) and double-crested cormorants (above).*

A rigorous triathlon and a December marathon (attracting about 3,500 runners each year) are available for more competitive athletes.

And if that's not enough, Kiawah Island lies just twenty-one miles from Charleston, "America's most beautifully preserved colonial city." Its beloved architecture, arts community, botanical gardens, parks, and array of shopping districts are toured year-round by crowds of admiring travelers.

Ospreys (above) routinely fish the lake that runs the length of Osprey Point's closing hole (below).

Sunset over Kiawah's dynamic marshlands

PINEHURST
RESORT & COUNTRY CLUB

Pinehurst Hotel has faithfully carried its timeless elegance into the resort's second century of existence.

James Walker Tufts wasn't even thinking about golf when he founded Pinehurst in 1895 on 5,000 acres of land in North Carolina's Sandhills region. It was his ambition to develop a winter sanctuary for New Englanders with breathing disorders, and to develop it so that people of modest means could afford to convalesce in comfort.

Tufts was the patriarch of a Massachusetts family. He started working at age sixteen as an apothecary, and by the age of twenty-one, he was the proprietor of three pharmacies. What most fascinated the young man, however, were soda fountains, and when he applied his imagination to the invention and manufacture of silver-plated marble soda fountains, he earned his fortune.

Although materially wealthy, Tuft s was never in the best of health. He was advised to forsake Massachusetts for a warmer, drier climate. The sprawling expanse of sand he would own in central North Carolina had been stripped of its timber, and was said to be extremely overpriced at one dollar per acre. He acquired the acreage regardless; the healing qualities of its soft, Southern breezes were priceless to Tufts.

Frederick Law Olmsted, designer of New York's Central Park, was commissioned to sketch out one of America's first planned municipalities. Pinehurst was to be a "village with open park spaces and winding streets that attain their usefulness by following lines of beauty." To achieve an atmosphere of unhurried neighborliness, Olmsted arranged the residential and commercial buildings around a village green, and then tied his community together with a maze of pedestrian lanes.

Within eighteen months, work crews had engineered the first phase of the resort: a delightful hotel, a small store, boarding houses, and several charming cottages.

Once botanists had determined which species might take hold in the thin soil, tens of thousands of trees and shrubs were painstakingly planted. Networks of paved streets were laid out, and a modern power plant and sewer system were installed. The Holly Inn, opened in 1895, boasted all the latest conveniences. Its electric lighting, steam heat, and telephones demonstrated that Tufts was intent on keeping up with the trends in hospitality. In 1901, his reputation as an innovator was further enhanced with the completion of the luxurious Carolina Hotel (which was renamed Pinehurst Hotel in the early 1970s).

While obliging others who, like himself, needed to winter in warmer climes, Tufts soon discovered that his guests deemed recreation to be a necessary therapy. He generously offered his patrons a choice of healthy pastimes: croquet, lawn bowling, trap shooting, tennis, and equine exercises.

The activity he found most intriguing, though, was the strange sight of those who spent their time strolling the resort's only grassy meadowland, hitting golf balls alongside grazing cows.

Pinehurst No. 2's 3rd hole

Striking examples of Donald Ross's artistry abound on No. 2's 5th hole.

In the late 1800s, golf was a comparatively new game in the United States, but Tufts immediately recognized its many benefits: it involved walking in the sunshine at one's own pace; it could be played by both men and women; it appealed to casual as well as competitive golfers; and it presented plenty of personal challenges.

Just as he had desired to be on the cutting edge of the hospitality industry, Tufts would seek the same position in recreation. Two years after breaking ground for Pinehurst, he revised the master plan and added a rudimentary nine-hole golf course. The enthusiastic response from guests confirmed his hunch that other facilities would be needed to satisfy the participants of this suddenly popular sport.

Tufts then heard about a young man who had left his home in Scotland (where he had apprenticed under St. Andrews' Old Tom Morris) after accepting the head professional position at Massachusetts' Oakley Country Club. Tufts didn't foresee a long future for the game he thought to be a fad. Still, he asked Donald Ross to serve as Pinehurst's golf pro during the winter months—Oakley's off-season. That simple invitation would forever alter the resort's mission. As the game's stature swelled, Pinehurst began to function more as a golf center and less as a health retreat; and Ross's prominence as a course designer began to spread worldwide.

It took very little time for Pinehurst to emerge as a golf destination worthy of hosting major tournaments for the game's premier players. It also took very little time for Pinehurst to burst at the seams from the demand for more golf. In fact, during the early 1900s, up to 15,000 people were being turned away each February and March, the area's high season.

The outstanding success of the resort's bluebird nesting box program (left, far left, and opposite page bottom) is evident throughout No. 2's woods.

No. 2's 12th hole

From the outset, Ross put his indelible stamp on the resort. Pinehurst's trademark was its unpretentious level of service; Ross's trademark was his unobtrusive style of architecture. His initial undertaking, though, did effect significant change to the landscape. When Ross first surveyed the property, there was not a single blade of grass on the resort course's tees and greens, which weren't the plush affairs they are today. Instead, hard-packed clay sufficed as a hole's starting point, and the sand putting surfaces were smoothed over by rags tied onto a broom handle.

Architects now have at their fingertips state-of-the-art machinery and technology to bulldoze, move, and grade acres of earth; to pump in millions of gallons of water; and to irrigate miles of lawn. Ross only employed brawny mules and men to prepare Pinehurst's barren-looking grounds for the introduction of the first patches of Bermuda grass.

Ross gave few interviews and spoke little about his courses, saying they would tell their own story, and in doing so, tell his as well.

Perfectly formed and placed bunkers defend No. 2's 14th green.

Tenacious bird-foot violets (below left)
and dwarf huckleberries (below right) poke through the matted pine straw of No. 2's 17th hole (above).

Ross's accomplishments exemplified understatement coupled with high standards. His golf courses are masters of minimalism, free of overbearing features and unspoiled by crass gimmickry. By 1910, he had immersed himself completely into the field of golf course design. His remarkable body of work includes Pinehurst Resort's first four courses, close to 400 others throughout North America, and one of the United States' original practice ranges—Pinehurst's famed "Maniac Hill."

344

The 5th hole on No. 5

The first nine holes of the world ranked No. 2 course were in play by 1901, lengthened in 1903, and integrated with the second nine in 1907. Ross then let it settle in for sixteen years before remodeling two more holes in 1923.

In the late '20s, the venerable Augusta National Golf Club began an intensive search for the architect who would create its "dream course." Ross was the leading candidate for the high-profile job, but after looking over Alister Mackenzie's Cypress Point in California, Augusta's Bobby Jones asked him to co-design with Mackenzie. Ross typically worked alone, made most decisions himself, and seldom suffered the suggestions of others. Believing his abilities were in question, he refused the offer and threw himself back into his beloved No. 2, determined to show off his prolific talents.

In 1935, Ross finished No. 2's metamorphosis, reconstructing some holes and re-routing a few others. Greens were newly contoured, crowned, seeded with grass, and surrounded with numerous humps and hollows.

Later that year, a young journalist visited Pinehurst and had the chance to meet and talk with Ross. The writer raved innocently about the course he had just toured in Augusta, prompting Ross to invite him to examine No. 2. They spent hours walking the layout, and as Ross revealed his approach to each hole, the reporter quickly realized that he was getting a rare glimpse into the mind of golf's great artisan.

Pinehurst's stylish clubhouse (above), sculpted tributes to Donald Ross and Richard Tufts (below left),
rustic Putterboy statuette (below right), manicured croquet lawns (opposite page bottom),
and wryly named "Maniac Hill" practice range (opposite page top) are just a few reminders of the resort's celebrated past.

In 1946, Ross touched up one more hole on No. 2, and in 1948, shortly after the resort's "favorite child" had staged the prestigious North and South Open, he died. Augusta National has since been fine-tuned by a dozen different architects, but Pinehurst claims that thirteen of No. 2's holes have remained virtually unchanged since 1935.

Some reviewers remark that No. 2 is "where the game has been and where it is going." Extreme golf course architecture ruled for a time, but gentler practitioners are steering their colleagues back to Donald Ross's principles of deceptive simplicity.

Bill Coore, a top contemporary designer, suggests it's the little things—the angles, contouring, and bunkering—that go together to make the whole greater than the sum of its parts. "So many golf holes today are based upon individual, dramatic elements," Coore states.

"The hole is an overwhelming ordeal, it's too dramatic." The genius of No. 2, he believes, is its quiet mystique that at first eludes players, then later confounds them with the choices that conjure up the element of doubt. "It lulls you into mistakes as opposed to bludgeoning you with them," he explains. "The theme runs throughout the story, but it's presented, then fades away, then is presented again. You build up and then soften, step back a ways, then set the tone for the next stage of development."

Donald Ross was friends with several members of the Tufts family, but most closely with Richard, grandson of the village's founder. Sharing a common dream, the two gentlemen confidently fashioned their home into one of the country's most desirable places to live. But regrettably, Pinehurst, "the dowager queen," could not avoid the disco era. In 1970, the third-generation Tufts sold their interest in Pinehurst to the Diamondhead Corporation, a land improvement company that promised to be an explosive force in the slow-paced county.

Horse-drawn carriage rides (opposite page) past the hotel's flowering dogwoods (top right) and massed azaleas (right) honor one of the resort's long-standing traditions.

Diamondhead increased its holdings to 10,000 acres, staked off 13,000 lots, and erected fifty split-level cottages and 200 condominiums. Marshall Park, the original village green, was a lush belt where the native flora of the Carolina Sandhills grew in profusion. Diamondhead felled its magnificent trees to build tennis courts, a racquet club, an ice-skating pavilion, bowling alleys, and a health spa. They redecorated the grand hotels to reflect the standard look of national franchise operations.

Those who had known and loved Pinehurst were in shock. Following Diamondhead's arrival, much of the village's warm, personal touch noticeably waned. The management and staff who had loyally represented the resort for years did not survive the takeover. However, Pinehurst's aging infrastructure had begun to crack at the edges. Even Diamondhead's harshest critics admitted that, while the steamroller approach was not appreciated, some of the upgrading was inevitable.

In its frantic ambition, Diamondhead overextended its financial resources, and in 1984, the property was secured by Club Resorts, Inc. From the very beginning, it was blissfully clear that the new owners were more interested in restoration rather than renovation. With its former shine and sophistication reinstated, the historical Pinehurst Resort & Country Club welcomed back familiar friends and eagerly greeted first-time guests.

The 17th hole on the No. 6 course traces the exhilarating rises and falls of the Carolina Sandhills.

The quiet setting of No. 7's 13th hole (above) attracts several of the area's eastern fox squirrels (below).

Charles Price, *Golf Magazine*'s pioneer editor and onetime reporter for the *Pinehurst Outlook,*

had this to say about the village's uncommon sincerity: "Pinehurst people don't try to outdo

each other with homes…they don't drive golf carts

with dry bars or Rolls-Royce grilles.

"They have no use for neon signs, bus tours, fat farms, nightclubs, stretch limos, outsized swimming pools, art galleries that insult your taste, antique shops full of bric-a-brac made a week ago, restaurants that award themselves three stars, or any of the confetti with which other golf resorts today carnivalize themselves."

The 15th on No. 7

A formidable island of sand fronts No. 7's par-three 16th green.

The allure of Moore County is supported by a consistent climate, swaying pine forests, and the cottage conservation of its residents and such local organizations as Weymouth Woods and the Sandhills Community College.

Indigenous sweet bay (opposite page bottom) and Venus' looking-glass (opposite page top) flowers bloom on the margins of No. 7's 17th hole (above).

Featuring formal gardens and natural ecosystems, the exquisite grounds of the college's Landscape Gardening building are maintained year-round for public viewing. The relaxing hideaway also functions as an outdoor classroom for the school's horticultural students.

Down the road, in Southern Pines, hikers are drawn to the tranquility of Weymouth Woods Sandhills Nature Preserve. The vital 425-acre timberland embraces North Carolina's last known stand of old growth longleaf pines, hardy populations of regional wildflowers, and scattered colonies of endangered red-cockaded woodpeckers.

Pinehurst at its century mark is again what it was—soft-spoken and eloquent. When it came time to select a location for the World Golf Hall of Fame, only Pinehurst would do as its home. Ben Hogan won his first professional tournament here. Chick Evans, Walter Hagen, Tommy Armour, Bobby Jones, Babe Zaharias, Gene Sarazen, Byron Nelson, Sam Snead, Gary Player, Jack Nicklaus, Arnold Palmer, Tom Watson, Ben Crenshaw, and Hale Irwin are just some of the champions who have sung the praises of Pinehurst.

Since its birth in 1895, the resort has evolved from owning a modest little nine-holer to operating eight highly acclaimed eighteen-hole layouts crafted by an elite group of golf course architects: Donald Ross, Ellis Maples, Robert Trent Jones, Sr., Rees Jones, and George and Tom Fazio.

The radiant Village Chapel (above) and colorful business core (opposite page) help to keep alive Pinehurst's famous New England spirit.

The 144 holes stretch for over thirty miles, and each year host more than 200,000 rounds of golf on the same turf trodden by the game's legends.

Opened in the spring of 1996, the Centennial – Pinehurst No. 8 course is soundly ushering the resort into the twenty-first century with its unwavering commitment to the ecology; and when Ronald Dodson, president and CEO of Audubon International, announced that the Tom Fazio creation had been chosen as an Audubon Signature Sanctuary, he added: "This commitment is the first step toward a more sustainable world."

Magnificent old estates lend an international flavor to the village of Pinehurst.

Brad Kocher and his grounds crew have teamed with the environmental consulting firm of Dr. J.H. Carter III & Associates, Inc. to carefully enhance, safeguard, and monitor the course's surprisingly broad array of native habitats. The 420-acre site has been thoughtfully transformed into a valuable refuge for the flora and fauna of the Sandhills region.

No. 8's 3rd hole

On its 100th anniversary in 1995, Pinehurst's directors pledged to never lose sight of the noble intention of James Walker Tufts: to remain at the forefront of destination resorts designed to rejuvenate world-weary visitors. This same exemplary attitude has defined Pinehurst Resort & Country Club's splendid past, and will most certainly guide its dynamic future.

The par-five 6th on No. 8

The 12th hole on Tom Fazio's No. 8 course is tightly flanked by a low-lying sandy barren.

Swamp honeysuckle (below left) and orange milkwort (below right) thrive on the marshy edges of No. 8's 8th hole (above).

A pristine wetland skirts the entire length of No. 8's 14th hole.

Ruddy ducks (below), wood ducks (above),
and mallard eggs (right) are living proof of the 14th hole's importance as a wildlife reserve.

Southern Pines' Weymouth Center is a long-time promoter and supporter of North Carolina's cultural arts and humanities.

The distinctive ecology of Weymouth Woods (below) is highlighted by low-growing clumps of staggerbush (above center) and dwarf iris (above left).

The spectacular theme gardens of the
Sandhills Community College (below and left) have been delighting visitors since 1978.

The college's elaborate boardwalk trail weaves
through a mature Sandhills forest (below) to a secluded pond occupied by a female bufflehead (below right).

Dissipating storm clouds over Lake Pinehurst capture the sunset's crimson afterglow.

THE HOMESTEAD

The historical retreat has proudly upheld Virginia's grand colonial traditions for well over two hundred years.

orth of the Blue Ridge, high in the Allegheny Mountains just inside Virginia's western border, a reader of maps will note place names that hint at the area's geological legacy. Rockbridge Baths, Falling Springs, Natural Well, Eagle Rock, White Sulphur Springs, Warm Springs, Healing Springs, and Hot Springs are all towns in or near Bath County, Virginia.

Blessed with rejuvenating waters, Bath County holds the imagination as a sanctuary where health and vigor are renewed, a haven where the spirit and soul are relaxed. For more than two centuries now, these desirable qualities have lured people to Hot Springs and its storied resort, The Homestead.

One of Hot Springs' favorite legends recalls an Indian brave's struggle to carry a message over the mountains to the tribes assembled by the ocean. Exhausted from his hurried trek through the peaks and passes of the Alleghenies, and endangered by the chill that follows a late spring nightfall, the brave looked about for the means of survival. In a steamy hollow ahead, he spied a glint of moonlight and followed it to a pool where he stooped to drink. The water was heated and the man was nearly frozen. He stepped into the shallow basin, and within seconds felt life returning to his icy fingers and toes. Upon reaching the tribal gathering a few days later, he told of the land and its magic waters which ran warm even when cold rains fell.

Published in an 1833 issue of *Southern Literary Messenger*, this story may be nothing more than fancy, but artifacts found at the springs at least prove that the natives were the first humans to discover and inhabit this secluded region.

In a journal authored in 1750 by Dr. Thomas Walker, the valley's waters are described to be "warmer than new milk." As word spread, access to the springs became a contentious issue as whites began to move in, recklessly laying claim to territory already occupied by the Indians.

In another diary entry, Walker unfairly reasoned that the natives were entirely to blame for the animosity between the two cultures. He felt that the abundant natural resources should have been shared only with the white travelers who came seeking the springs.

The Alleghenies' pitching foothills shape The Cascades' 7th hole.

An eastern kingbird (below left) and a Brewer's blackbird (below right) scrutinize play at The Cascades' par-three 8th hole (above).

Towering sugar maples stand guard on the fringes of The Cascades' 12th hole.

Around 1740, the valley containing the magic waters was surveyed and colonized by Scottish and Irish immigrants. Positioned on the colonies' western front, the location served as a strategic waypoint between the fortresses built to secure the newly appropriated Indian lands.

In 1755, George Washington (then a colonel in the Virginia militia) journeyed to the area on an inspection tour of these fortifications. During the stay, Washington and his entourage repeatedly sampled the valley's three primary hot pools which bubbled up from the Earth's depths: Warm Springs, Healing Springs, and Hot Springs.

The natural wildflower gardens of The Cascades' 14th hole (below) support gorgeous arrangements of yellow lady's slippers (above right) and large-flowered trilliums (above left).

The Cascades' par-three 15th

Warm Springs was first to capitalize on people's quest for relief from pain and sickness. In 1751, land title was granted to John Lewis, the gentleman who headed the effort to construct the men's bathhouse in 1761. Still open for business, the exquisite wooden masterpiece was designed by Thomas Jefferson, the revered American statesman and frequent Warm Springs visitor.

Once the threat of Indian uprisings had ended, the matter of obliging pilgrims began to nag the valley's residents. Unannounced strangers, in need of food and rest after negotiating rugged mountain passes, arrived almost daily.

The adventurous 16th hole is protected from tee to green by the pervasive Cascades Stream.

Thomas Bullitt was one such beleaguered local. Now that a bathhouse had been established, the crowds continued to swell throughout the district. Constant requests for lodging frustrated Bullitt, but ultimately planted an enterprising notion in his head: why not build a guest house to accommodate the callers? In 1766, his hostelry opened its doors, initiating a two-century succession of refinement for one of the United States' premier resorts: The Homestead.

The Cascades' palatial clubhouse (above) watches over the course's par-three closing hole (below).

Vigorous clumps of showy orchis (below right) and speckled wood lilies (below left) edge a breathtaking section of the resort's Cascades Gorge (above).

While Bullitt had the right idea, it was Dr. Thomas Goode—a physician with connections to an influential Virginia family—who had the savvy and credentials to effectively promote the resort once he acquired it in 1832. Some would call it clever marketing and others would call it snake oil, but when Dr. Goode declared that the waters at his Hot Springs spa would cure anyone of anything, it was as if the Messiah had spoken.

Warm Springs had been designated as the seat of Bath County in 1791, but Hot Springs soon eclipsed its neighboring town in economic growth, spurred on by Dr. Goode's very fashionable pronouncements regarding the virtues of The Homestead's mineral water pools. Additional amenities were geared not toward the ill and infirm, but to resorters looking to escape the humid East Coast summers.

In 1836, Warm Springs opened up a bathhouse reserved exclusively for female patrons. Situated next to the men's shelter, the women's facility was often utilized by Mrs. Robert E. Lee. To assist the genteel lady, a device consisting of a chair on a platform was employed to lower her into the pool, as it was thought the best way to receive benefit from the water was to remain inactive while submerged.

Eastern box turtles (opposite page bottom) and tremendous waterfalls (above and opposite page top) highlight guided explorations of the Cascades Gorge.

Farther downstream, bunches of fire pinks (below right) and Bowman's root (below left) flourish alongside The Lower Cascades' 6th hole (above).

The Lower Cascades #7

By 1838, the area was attracting over 5,000 vacationers a year. In 1846, Dr. Goode increased

the capacity of his hotel and personally directed it to a position of great prominence.

The Lower Cascades #13

When Dr. Goode died in 1858, people were still riding stagecoaches through craggy mountain passes to reach the remote valley. Bath County's isolation, however, may have been its saving grace during the Civil War.

Converted into hospitals for Confederate soldiers, the county's resorts were buffered from the heaviest fighting—all three survived the devastating war, suffering only minor damages.

In 1891, a syndicate of Chesapeake & Ohio Railway Company stockholders bought up Warm Springs Valley's spas and some 4,700 acres of mountain terrain.

Thickets dotted with star chickweed (above right) and sessile bellwort (above left) edge The Lower Cascades' picturesque 14th hole (below).

386

Under the discerning eye of its new owners, The Homestead began to dress up. The property was landscaped with miles of riding and hiking trails; eleven cottages (dubbed Cottage Row) were erected; and tennis courts and a six-hole golf course were set into the rolling countryside. Finally, a European-style spa and The Casino building were developed.

The long climb to The Lower Cascades' 17th green is rewarded by all-encompassing views of the course's spectacular alpine setting.

At the hotel, a sheltered pond (above) and its resident woodchuck (below) complement the East Wing's grounds.

To better serve the thriving hospitality industry, the railway syndicate had a C & O branch line from Covington up and running by 1892. Now the springs were more convenient to the people who craved the therapeutic waters.

Gray catbirds (above) and northern mockingbirds (top) beg for handouts from The Casino's diners.

The vintage Casino building is a favorite gathering place for The Homestead's guests.   COURTESY OF THE HOMESTEAD

Yet another new beginning for Hot Springs occurred on July 2, 1901, when the beloved Homestead hotel complex burned to the ground. In three hours, a century and a half of elegance was erased—only The Spa, The Casino, and Cottage Row were spared.

Resort directors wasted no time whatsoever. The day after the fire, architects were brought in to plan out a grand new hotel. In March of 1902, the main section of the red brick, Georgian-style edifice was finished. The following year, the West Wing was opened and connected to The Spa via a splendid breezeway. With its familiar blend of Southern charm and colonial presence firmly reinstated, The Homestead's guest list grew steadily over the next decade, prompting construction of the East Wing in 1914.

The '20s became a period of prosperity for the entire valley. The Homestead managed its own dairy and poultry farms to keep its kitchens and dining rooms supplied. At Healing Springs, the resort purchased several adjacent farms and estates, enabling it to spread its wings yet wider. On Warm Springs Mountain, a runway was put down to receive those who preferred air travel.

Just before the '30s came crashing in on the American economy, The Homestead's administrators decided that more guest rooms were needed, so the old ballroom was razed and replaced with a landmark million-dollar structure known as the Tower.

Idyllic homes (top) and churches (center and right) reflect the easygoing pace of Hot Springs.

The Old Course #8

It was a classic case of bad timing: the Great Depression critically curbed hotel bookings as vast fortunes were lost almost overnight. The Virginia Hot Springs Co., holding company for The Homestead, declared bankruptcy in 1938.

Vibrant sundrops (below left) and violet wood sorrels (below right) enhance the dense forests of The Old Course's 13th hole (above).

By 1940, the company was reorganized into a corporation, only to face another fiscal crisis as World War II escalated. Following the war, however, The Homestead's cash flows took a sharp upturn, thanks in part to the spiraling popularity of the game of golf (first played in the United States in 1887, and at The Homestead five years after that).

In 1912, The Old Course—the resort's original six-holer—was wonderfully redesigned and stretched out to eighteen holes by Donald J. Ross, arguably the most brilliant golf course architect of all time. Ross was careful, though, not to alter the first tee, which back then and still today is the country's oldest in continuous use.

When the financial boom of the 1920s gave rise to a fresh generation of leisure-seekers, it quickly became obvious that one golf course couldn't handle the mounting demand.

The scenery of The Old Course's 17th hole is dominated by The Homestead's gleaming Tower.

Widely regarded as the nation's finest mountain layout, The Cascades Golf Course was conceived by William S. Flynn in the first half of the '20s. Since its debut in 1924, The Cascades has compiled some pretty impressive honors. In 1996, it was named number one in Virginia, number thirty-nine in America, number seventy-six in the world, one of the eight top experiences in non-private golf, and the third best resort course in the country.

Known for its severly tilted fairways and swift flowing stream, The Cascades is a mecca of sorts for golfers of all sorts. It was featured in *Golf for Women* as one of America's most "women friendly" courses; it received the "Greens of Distinction" award from *Corporate & Incentive Travel*; and it earned the "Gold Tee" award from *Meetings & Conventions*.

Just north of the hotel, Warm Springs' glorious past is faithfully preserved by its venerable courthouse (top) and inviting bathhouses (right).

In the early '60s, Robert Trent Jones, Sr. was appointed to design The Lower Cascades Golf Course. Routing holes along the valley floor and over the foothills of the lush acreage, his strapping creation was ready for the resort's golfers by 1963.

Together, the three exceptional courses have challenged many of the game's greatest players with a number of nationally-ranked tournaments.

Bath County flaunts its famous pastoral colors from spring (below) through fall (opposite page).

In fact, Sam Snead, professional golf's most prolific champion, was born and raised just a few miles from the hotel. Shortly before the start of his touring career, Snead even worked for The Homestead as an assistant pro.

Throughout its history, The Homestead has demonstrated an uncanny ability to attract folks from all walks of life. Among the resort's more notable guests were war heroes Robert E. Lee and George C. Marshall; industrialists Henry Ford, John D. Rockefeller, and Cornelius Vanderbilt; politicians Taft, Wilson, McKinley, Coolidge, and Johnson as well as Franklin D. Roosevelt, Nixon, Ford, Reagan, and Eisenhower; the Duke and Duchess of Windsor; and inventor Thomas Edison.

COURTESY OF THE HOMESTEAD

THE HOMESTEAD: CHAPTER 17

Furthering its reputation as an innovator, The Homestead pioneered the South's skiing industry in the late 1950s. Sepp Kober was called upon to fashion a variety of runs down the slopes of the Alleghenies which loomed over the hotel. Endowed with such technological marvels as snow guns and an uphill trestle car lift, Kober's magnificent ski facility soon transformed The Homestead into a four-season vacation destination.

For more than 230 years, Warm Springs Valley has been harnessed by men who understood its commercial potential. As the county contributed its natural resources to the profit margin, care was taken not to exhaust those resources or lose sight of Mother Nature's appeal to city-dwelling visitors.

In 1994, a five-year, multimillion dollar expansion and restoration project was launched by The Homestead's diligent new owner, Club Resorts, Inc.; and when the carefully engineered work is completed, none of the ridges and gorges which lend their primal beauty to this extraordinary setting will have been disturbed.

COURTESY OF THE HOMESTEAD

*Carved out of the pristine wilderness between Covington and Hot Springs,
the Jackson River spills over Falling Springs' jagged rock face (above and opposite page).*

The Jackson River's rugged course (above) is softened by striking collections of pink lady's slippers (below left) and Jack-in-the-pulpits (below right).

As the legendary warrior learned centuries earlier, this shimmering retreat possesses the power to revive weary travelers. With this at the heart of the resort's mission, it's easy to imagine this 15,000-acre treasure enduring well into its third century.

399

Glimpses of Virginia's celebrated natural and cultural histories are dramatically revealed from the resort's Sunset Hill.

THE HOMESTEAD: CHAPTER 17

CALLAWAY GARDENS

Native azaleas, pines, and flagstones grace the serene walkways of the Ida Cason Callaway Memorial Chapel.

Authentic landscape is not easily formed. The natural origins of most terrain was played out so long ago that no eyes were present to behold the process.

Today, entrepreneurs and architects with sufficient financing and the right equipment can effect their own landscape evolution. The carving of rivers and the shaping of mountains which took place over millions of years can now occur on a smaller scale within a few days.

People build for many reasons. It's done to earn a living, to satisfy an urge of the ego, and even to show respect for nature's creations.

This latter desire is what led to the founding of Georgia's magnificent Callaway Gardens. Now drawing more than one million visitors annually, the Gardens were conceived in the early 1950s by Cason J. Callaway and his wife, Virginia Hand Callaway.

A textile manufacturer by trade, Cason's deep affinity for the outdoors was shared completely with Virginia. From their numerous treks into the Pine Mountain region of Harris County, they cultivated a keen admiration for its fragile plant and animal communities. One location in particular delighted the Callaways. This rare piece of earth featured sporadic clumps of delicate plumleaf azaleas (which grow wild only in the Pine Mountain area) and a cool, crystalline pool known as Blue Springs.

In 1930, Cason purchased a 2,500-acre parcel in Harris County that included Blue Springs as well as an old, depleted cotton plantation. Needing to escape the pressures of the textile mills, Cason gradually increased his land holdings to 40,000 acres and made plans for the establishment of a farming operation. His Blue Springs Farm became a forerunner in Georgia's agricultural industry, experimenting with such innovative ideas as terracing (to reduce erosion), fertilizers and cover crops (to replenish the soil), and supplementary crops (to increase profits).

Upper Falls Creek Lake reflects the dramatic setting and stern challenge of Mountain View's 15th hole.

With considerable input from Mrs. Callaway, lavish gardens were designed to decorate the property with both native and non-native flowers. A long-practicing horticulturist, Virginia lovingly nurtured the plots along with her friends' appreciation for them. The Callaways embodied what philosopher and ecologist Aldo Leopold called the "Land Ethic."

Hoping to develop a place where people could come to commune with nature, they took on the mammoth task of replanting the bare fields with over 200,000 trees and shrubs. Once the undertaking was completed, and upon deeding 14,000 acres to the Ida Cason Callaway Foundation, their hope came to fruition with the opening of Callaway Gardens in 1952.

Mountain View #3

CALLAWAY GARDENS: CHAPTER 18

Edging Mountain View's par-three 12th green (above),
the shoreline of Upper Falls Creek Lake is routinely visited by great egrets (opposite page top) and Florida cooters (opposite page bottom).

Cason and Virginia worked tirelessly to supply their guests with everything from quiet meditative spots to rousing sporting pursuits to exciting educational programs. Its mission, "to provide a wholesome environment where all may find beauty, relaxation, inspiration, and a better understanding of the living world," is an ongoing priority at Callaway Gardens.

Since the initial theme behind Callaway's formation was horticulture, a great deal of its resources are committed to that very subject. For the benefit of its patrons, an inviting network of walking paths access the Gardens' dazzling arrangements of indigenous and introduced flora.

Springtime renews these tranquil destinations, and in the early part of this enchanting season, the Azalea Trail and its Overlook Garden are Callaway's showiest outdoor theaters. Flourishing beneath giant pines, close to 700 varieties of azaleas dress up the grounds with staggering quantities of colored blossoms.

Each May, the Rhododendron Trail explodes with the sights and fragrances of the seventy-plus species which border its winding, wooded footpaths.

Billed as the world's most diverse public collection, the Holly Trail encompasses nearly 500 cultivars of American, English, and Oriental hollies; Japanese camellias, tea olives, and barberries lend their own unique accents to the mix.

The Wildflower Trail flaunts its natural assets all year-long. Filtered sunlight reveals the flora of each season in a variety of settings, including meadow, woodland, and wetland habitats.

Next to the Wildflower Trail's entrance, the Pioneer Log Cabin serves to remind people of the area's rustic past. The 170-year-old homestead was accidentally discovered just north of Callaway Gardens, in Troup County. Anxious to exhibit the finding, Cason had the weathered dwelling relocated to the Gardens and filled with period furnishings and tools. Interpreting the log cabin's history is just one of the many duties assigned to the Callaway Gardens Education Department.

Mountain Creek Walking Trail lazily traces Mountain Creek Lake and its populations of turtles, songbirds, egrets, herons, ducks, and geese.

The Laurel Springs Trail leads hikers into an Appalachian hardwood forest thick with mountain laurel and sweet bay. The tangled, uneven route traverses Pine Mountain's rugged slopes, weeping springs, and outcroppings of Hollis quartzite—the richly textured stone that embellishes a number of the Gardens' buildings, including the Callaway Country Store and the Ida Cason Callaway Memorial Chapel.

People are encouraged to heed the advice at Callaway's gate: "Take nothing from these gardens except nourishment for the soul, consolation for the heart, and inspiration for the mind."

The Azalea Trail ushers in spring with millions of hybrid azalea flowers. Courtesy of Callaway Gardens

Occupying more than seven acres and growing over 400 varieties of vegetables, fruits, herbs, and flowers, Mr. Cason's Vegetable Garden was the last major project launched by Cason. Following conventional erosion control practices, plantings are spread across three large terraces.

Closer to the Overlook Garden, cultivated azalea bushes (top)
are interspersed with such treasured natives as Piedmont (above left) and Florida (above right) species.

Standout plots include: the Home Demonstration Garden, the Southern host for the PBS television series, *The Victory Garden*; an All-American Test Garden, where trial vegetables and flowers are evaluated against national results; the Butterfly Garden; and a fragrant herb bed wrapped around an analemmatic sundial.

Adjacent to the Azalea Trail, Whippoorwill Lake (below) helps to feed the resort's green herons (above).

410

The Cecil B. Day Butterfly Center has been astounding visitors since 1988. Construction of the building—named for the late founder of Days Inns of America—was initiated by a generous lead grant presented to Callaway Gardens by Cecil's widow, Deen Day Smith.

Striking Oconee azaleas (top left), obedient plants (top right), hibiscus blossoms (bottom left), and holly bushes (bottom right) adorn the Wildflower Trail.

Distinguished as North America's largest glass-enclosed tropical butterfly house, it accommodates up to 1,000 vibrant specimens. The winged creatures flutter freely throughout the jungle-like environment, sustained by cut fruit and the nectar of exotic flowers.

The remarkable conservatory boasts 854 glass panels, an indoor waterfall and stream, outdoor butterfly gardens, and an attached lobby that supports atop its roof a vintage cupola salvaged from Virginia Hand Callaway's childhood home.

The Pioneer Log Cabin (below) and its costumed hostess (above) evoke images of a bygone era.

The fertile acreage of Mr. Cason's Vegetable Garden (above) is highlighted by an ivy-covered gazebo (below left) and rows of ripening muscadine grapes (below right).

413

Advancing art and education are two important objectives of the Butterfly Center. Its gallery contains a selection of butterfly watercolors by Chevalier de Freminville—a nineteenth-century French artist—as well as a number of illustrations by John Abbot—a pioneer naturalist who lived in Georgia from 1776 to 1840. Informational displays identify resident butterflies, an orientation theater screens a film detailing the life cycle and significance of a butterfly, and workshops are run to help people attract the insects to their own gardens.

Just east of the Vegetable Garden, Rob Sinkler and Stacy Liner direct a fascinating birds of prey exhibition during Callaway Gardens' Spring Celebration.

The John A. Sibley Horticultural Center commemorates a man who was a close friend of the Callaways, a trustee of the Ida Cason Callaway Foundation, and a renowned Georgian lawyer, banker, and civic leader. The modern five-acre complex is endowed with 30,000 square feet of production greenhouses, 20,000 square feet of interior show space, a twenty-two-foot waterfall, and a spectacular outdoor park. A bank of oversized folding glass doors are open from spring to fall, seamlessly linking the inside and outside worlds.

The contemporary look of the Cecil B. Day Butterfly Center (below) is beautifully contrasted by its turn-of-the-century cupola (above).

Heliconius hecale

Hypolimnas bolina

Neptis hylas

The Horticultural Center is a model of energy efficiency. For example, temperature extremes are moderated by shading, venting, insulating, and evaporation operations; solar radiation is absorbed by 300 tons of Tennessee flagstone; and a massive glass block wall lets in light but keeps out heat and cold.

In 1962, Norman Vincent Peale officially opened the Ida Cason Callaway Memorial Chapel. Dedicated to Cason's mother, the beloved chapel is utilized for summer and Easter services, organ recitals, weddings, christenings, and even private prayers and meditations.

Like most structures at Callaway Gardens, the chapel was built with primarily indigenous materials: the heavy wooden beams were hewn from local timber; the walls are Hollis quartzite; the floor is north Georgia Cherokee flagstone; and the altar is a Pine Mountain boulder. A series of ornate stained-glass windows depict the four seasons, a hardwood forest of the Piedmont region, and typical evergreen pines of the coastal plain.

416

Falls Creek Lake lies at the foot of the chapel, reflecting back its timeless English Gothic architecture. The graceful house of worship is a fitting tribute to the woman who instilled in Cason the firm spiritual convictions which were the pillars of his life.

Interior sections of the John A. Sibley Horticultural Center feature elegant floral arrangements (above) and a waterfall-misted plant rockery (left).

Callaway Gardens entertains its guests with a year-round assortment of activities. Robin Lake Beach, one of the country's largest man-made beaches, is an especially busy place during the spring and summer.

The Horticultural Center's courtyard (below) is a colorful refuge for brown thrashers (above left) and eastern tiger swallowtails (above right).

Each April through August, the lake stages a number of exclusive events, including Florida State University's "Flying High" Circus, a water-ski competition, an Independence Day celebration, and special music concerts. Excursions aboard the Robin E. Lee Paddlewheeler treat vacationers to one of the South's most romantic nineteenth-century legacies.

The Ida Cason Callaway Memorial Chapel (above and opposite page) has been enchanting visitors since 1962.

Other lakes on the property are popular with those who enjoy spin casting and fly-fishing for bass, bream, and trout. A catch-and-release policy, professional guides, group clinics, personal instruction, and the Callaway Fly Fishing Shop virtually guarantee successful outings.

The 7.5-mile Discovery Bicycle Trail, a fitness center, and tennis and racquetball courts are available for more rigorous workouts.

However, the principal recreational activity at Callaway Gardens—and major revenue generator—is its sixty-three holes of golf.

In keeping with the long-standing philosophy of the resort, the golf courses were precisely arranged to take full advantage of Callaway's extraordinary scenery.

Lake View's 12th (below) and 11th (opposite page) holes are tightly enclosed by the resort's signature hardwoods and evergreens.

J.B. McGovern and Dick Wilson each created nine of Lake View's holes, Callaway's original
golf course. Before commencing construction, both men promised that the site's pristine lakes
and forests would be carefully blended into their designs.

Lake View #13

True to their word, aesthetics and shot values were brilliantly integrated: the lakes which silently mirror their botanical landscapes also protect seven of the course's holes.

Gardens View was fashioned by noted architect Joe Lee in 1969. Its lush green fairways roll gently past swaying pines, healthy orchards, and even a sprawling vineyard laden with Callaway's famous muscadine grapes.

Sky View, the resort's nine-hole executive course, is an ideal practice ground for the short shots as well as a favorite venue for family gatherings.

In the fall, Mountain View hosts some of the game's top players during the Buick Challenge, a PGA Tour® event. The big, brawny layout—also a Dick Wilson design—is set into a towering Georgia pine forest undergrown with hardy bunches of flowering dogwoods.

The purple martins (above) living next to Lake View's 5th green (below) are in charge of controlling Mountain Creek Lake's insect populations.

The opening hole at Gardens View drops steadily into the resort's mature pine groves.

Mountain View is soundly defended by formidable elevation changes, strategically positioned bunkers, and perplexing putting surfaces—features which demand the very best from its amateur and professional golfers alike.

All of Callaway's main attractions are conveniently located along Scenic Drive, a looping roadway that leisurely explores the entire acreage.

In the tradition of the Callaway Foundation, approximately 600 volunteers keep the vision alive and growing. These folks garden, greet guests, provide clerical support, and generally help fulfill the Callaways' dream "that everyone should have access to beauty that lifts the spirit."

Gardens View #11

Located a few miles from the resort, the FDR State Park office functions as an interpretive center for the area's hikers.

In the peaceful woods and gardens of western Georgia, this dream has taken root and become reality for millions of visitors.

South of the Gardens' main entrance, the Callaway Country Store serves up tastes of rural Georgia.

Within FDR State Park, a breathless overlook on Pine Mountain's ridge line watches the sun sink through a hazy Georgia sky.

Amelia Island Plantation
    P.O. Box 3000
    Amelia Island, Florida 32035
    1-800-874-6878
    1-904-261-6161

The American Club/Blackwolf Run
    Highland Drive
    Kohler, Wisconsin 53044
    1-800-344-2838
    1-920-457-8000

The BALSAMS Grand Resort Hotel
    Dixville Notch, New Hampshire 03576
    1-800-255-0600
    1-603-255-3400

The Boulders
    P.O. Box 2090
    Carefree, Arizona 85377
    1-800-553-1717
    1-602-488-9009

Boyne USA Resorts
    P.O. Box 19
    Boyne Falls, Michigan 49713
    1-800-462-6963
    1-616-549-2441

Callaway Gardens
    P.O. Box 2000
    Pine Mountain, Georgia 31822
    1-800-225-5292
    1-706-663-2281

Chateau Whistler Resort
    4599 Chateau Boulevard
    Whistler, British Columbia V0N 1B4
    1-800-606-8244
    1-604-938-8000

Eagle Ridge Inn & Resort
    P.O. Box 777
    Galena, Illinois 61036
    1-800-892-2269
    1-815-777-2444

The Equinox
    Historic Route 7A
    Manchester Village, Vermont 05254
    1-800-362-4747
    1-802-362-4700

Grand View Lodge
    South 134 Nokomis
    Nisswa, Minnesota 56468
    1-800-432-3788
    1-218-963-2234

Highlands Links/Keltic Lodge
    Middle Head Peninsula
    Ingonish Beach, Nova Scotia B0C 1L0
    1-800-565-0444
    1-902-285-2880

The Homestead
    P.O. Box 2000
    Hot Springs, Virginia 24445
    1-800-336-5771
    1-540-839-1766

The Inn and Links at Spanish Bay
    2700 17-Mile Drive
    Pebble Beach, California 93953
    1-800-654-9300
    1-831-624-3811

Kiawah Island Resort
    12 Kiawah Beach Drive
    Kiawah Island, South Carolina 29455
    1-800-654-2924
    1-843-768-2121

Pinehurst Resort & Country Club
    P.O. Box 4000
    Pinehurst, North Carolina 28374
    1-800-487-4653
    1-910-295-6811

The Resort Semiahmoo
    9565 Semiahmoo Parkway
    Blaine, Washington 98230
    1-800-770-7992
    1-360-371-2000

Sunriver Resort
    P.O. Box 3609
    Sunriver, Oregon 97707
    1-800-547-3922
    1-541-593-1000

Wintergreen Resort
    P.O. Box 706
    Wintergreen, Virginia 22958
    1-800-325-2200
    1-804-325-2200

BIBLIOGRAPHY

Abrahamson, Eric. *Historic Monterey: California's Forgotten First Capital*. Santa Barbara, Calif.: Sequoia Communications, 1989.

Alderton, David. *Turtles & Tortoises of the World*. New York: Facts on File, Inc., 1988.

Bale, Florence G. *Historic Galena: Yesterday and Today Since 1820*. Galena, Ill.: L.M. Harbin, 1939.

Banfield, A.W.F. *The Mammals of Canada*. Toronto: University of Toronto Press, 1977.

Bath County Chamber of Commerce. *The County of Bath: 1996/97 Visitors Guide*. Hot Springs, Va.: Bath County Chamber of Commerce, 1996.

BC Parks. *Garibaldi Provincial Park*. Brackendale, B.C.: BC Parks, 1995.

Carter, David. *Eyewitness Handbooks Butterflies and Moths*. Toronto: Stoddart Publishing Co. Limited, 1992.

Chaplin, Lois Trigg. *The Story of Callaway Gardens*. Birmingham, Ala.: Icon Graphics, 1991.

Conant, Roger, and Joseph T. Collins. *Peterson Field Guides, Reptiles and Amphibians: Eastern/Central North America*. Boston: Houghton Mifflin Company, 1991.

Equinox Preservation Trust. *Equinox Preservation Trust Trail Guide*. Manchester Village, Vt.: Equinox Preservation Trust, 1994.

Gordon, John. *The Great Golf Courses of Canada*. Toronto: McGraw-Hill Ryerson Limited, 1991.

Hait, Pam, and Jerry Jacka. *The Spirit of The Boulders: A Desert Romance*. Carefree, Ariz.: The Boulders, 1988.

Jaccard, Deon L. *Clash of the Cultures: The Awakening of History for Amelia Island, Florida*. Amelia Island: Amelia Island Museum of History, 1992.

Kohler Foundation, Inc. *The Waelderhaus*. Kohler, Wisc.: Kohler Foundation, Inc., n.d..

Leland, John G. *A History of Kiawah Island*. Charleston: Kiawah Island Company, 1977.

Lewis, Phebe Ann. *The Equinox: Historic Home of Hospitality*. Manchester, Vt.: Johnny Appleseed Bookshop, 1993.

Lothian, W.F. *A Brief History of Canada's National Parks*. Ottawa: Minister of Environment Canada/Minister of Supply and Services Canada, 1987.

Mattison, Chris. *Lizards of the World*. New York: Facts on File, Inc., 1989.

McCallen, Brian. *Golf Resorts of the World: The Best Places to Stay and Play*. New York: Harry N. Abrams, Inc., 1993.

McClurken, James M. *Gah-Baen-Jhagwah-Buk—The Way it Happened: A Visual Culture History of the Little Traverse Bay Bands of Odawa*. East Lansing, Mich.: Michigan State University Museum, 1991.

Michigan Department of Natural Resources. *Michigan State Parks*. Lansing, Mich.: Michigan Department of Natural Resources, 1996.

Niering, William, A., and Nancy C. Olmstead. *National Audubon Society Field Guide to North American Wildflowers: Eastern Region*. 15th ed. New York: Alfred A. Knopf, 1995.

Pebble Beach Company. *1994–1995 Pebble Beach Company Environmental Annual Report*. Pebble Beach, Calif.: Pebble Beach Company, 1995.

Pebble Beach Company. *Pebble Beach Nature Trails*. Pebble Beach, Calif.: Pebble Beach Company, 1995.

Pebble Beach Company. *The Del Monte Forest: An Informal History*. Pebble Beach, Calif.: Pebble Beach Company, 1984.

Peterson, Roger Tory. *Peterson Field Guides: Eastern Birds*. 4th ed. Boston: Houghton Mifflin Company, 1980.

Point Lobos Natural History Association. *Point Lobos State Reserve: A Living Museum*. Carmel, Calif.: Point Lobos Natural History Association, 1983.

Porcher, Richard D. *Wildflowers of the Carolina Lowcountry and Lower Pee Dee*. Columbia, S.C.: University of South Carolina Press, 1995.

Runtz, Michael. *Wild Things: The Hidden World of Animals*. Erin, Ont.: The Boston Mills Press, 1995.

Spellenberg, Richard. *National Audubon Society Field Guide to North American Wildflowers: Western Region*. 15th ed. New York: Alfred A. Knopf, 1995.

Stewart, Darryl. *The North American Animal Almanac*. Toronto: General Publishing Co. Limited, 1984.

Stokes, Donald, and Lillian Stokes. *Stokes Field Guide to Birds: Western Region*. Boston: Little, Brown and Company, 1996.

Sunriver Properties of Oregon, Ltd. *Sunriver: Historical Highlights 1855–1993*. Sunriver, Ore.: Sunriver Properties of Oregon, Ltd., n.d.

The BALSAMS Grand Resort Hotel. *Dixville Notch Natural History Handbook*. Dixville Notch, N.H.: The BALSAMS Grand Resort Hotel, 1992.

Wintergreen Resort. *Outdoor Program Hiking Guide*. Wintergreen, Va.: Wintergreen Resort, 1993.

Zapffe, Carl A. *Oldtimers: Stories of Our Pioneers*. Brainerd, Minn.: Echo Publishing and Printing, Inc., 1987.

I Will Never Write A Love Poem

by Jaime DiPietro

I have felt the desert
at night, laying on land
rich with tradition
and legend, warm winds
and coyotes singing me to sleep,
but I will never write a love poem.

I have stood on mountaintops,
touching the sky, blue
and vast, with smiles
and sweat, my body stronger
and wiser, glowing with light,
but I will never write a love poem.

I have sailed many seas,
with the sun rising
around me, promising
the greatness of another day,
safe in Her womb of sky and sea,
but I will never write a love poem.

I have heard your whispers
with the lights out,
desire kissing my lips, and
in your arms I crave deserts,
mountaintops, and the endless sea,
and I will never write a love poem.